FERDINAND DENNIS

Ferdinand Dennis was born in Jamaica but brought up and educated in Britain. He is widely experienced as a journalist and his BBC Radio 4 series 'Journey Round My People', which formed the genesis for this book, has been highly praised. He is also the author of BEHIND THE FRONTLINES; A JOURNEY INTO AFRO-BRITAIN, which won the 1988 Martin Luther King Memorial Prize, a novel, THE SLEEPLESS SUMMER, and short stories which have been published in magazines as well as broadcast on BBC Radio 4. Recently he has co-edited a survey of the 75-year history of the magazine *West Africa*.

In 1991, Ferdinand Dennis was made an Honorary Research Fellow at Birkbeck College. He lives in London.

Ferdinand Dennis

BACK TO AFRICA

A Journey

Copyright © 1992 by Ferdinand Dennis

First published in Great Britain in 1992 by Sceptre Books

A Sceptre original

Sceptre is an imprint of Hodder and Stoughton Paperbacks, a division of Hodder and Stoughton Ltd

British Library C.I.P.

Dennis, Ferdinand
  Back to Africa: Journey
  I. Title
  916.604

  ISBN 0-340-57962-5

Printed and bound in Great Britain for Hodder and Stoughton Paperbacks, a division of Hodder and Stoughton Ltd, Mill Road, Dunton Green, Sevenoaks, Kent TN13 2YA. (Editorial Office: 47 Bedford Square, London WC1B 3DP) by Clays Ltd, St Ives plc. Photoset by Rowland Phototypesetting Ltd, Bury St Edmunds, Suffolk.

For my children, Efua & Nike

CONTENTS

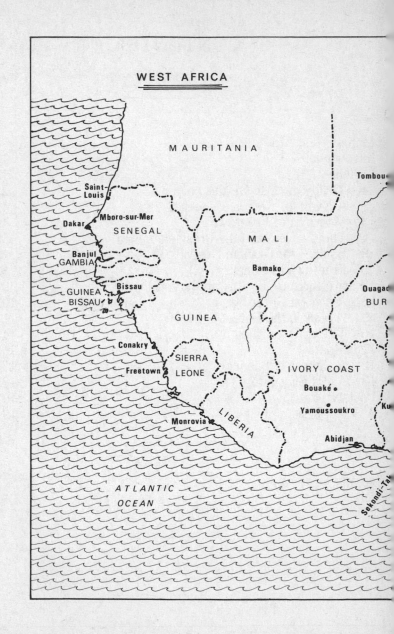

WEST AFRICA

MAURITANIA

Tombou

Saint-
Louis

Mboro-sur-Mer

Dakar   SENEGAL

M A L I

Banjul
GAMBIA

Bamako

Bissau

Ouagad
BUR

GUINEA
BISSAU

GUINEA

Conakry

SIERRA
LEONE

IVORY COAST

Freetown

Bouaké

Yamoussoukro   Ku

Monrovia   LIBERIA

Abidjan

A T L A N T I C

O C E A N

Sekondi-Tak

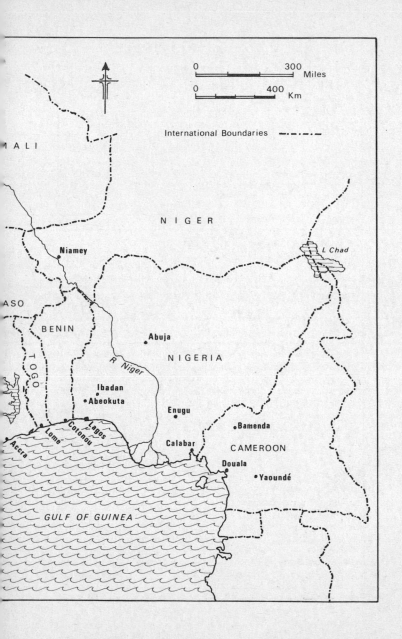

| 0 | | 300 | Miles |
| 0 | | 400 | Km |

International Boundaries — · — · —

MALI

NIGER

Niamey

ASO

BENIN

TOGO

Abuja

R Niger

NIGERIA

Ibadan
Abeokuta

Lagos
Cotonou
Lome
Accra

Enugu

Calabar

Bamenda

CAMEROON

Douala

Yaoundé

L Chad

GULF OF GUINEA

INTRODUCTION

My perceptions of Africa and Africans have undergone many changes over the years. Throughout my London childhood I devoured comic books, boys' adventure stories and films which portrayed Africa as a dark, vast continent inhabited by cannibalistic, half-naked savages whose *raison d'être* appeared to be to act as servile porters for White missionaries and intrepid explorers, and bewildered spectators or grateful beneficiaries of Tarzan's benign exploits. These Africans all seemed to be stricken with aphasia; they grunted, yelled, whooped, screamed; rolled their eyes like chameleons, or bared their teeth in parodic attempts at communication. Naturally, I completely and unquestioningly identified with the White heroes, whether it was the incredible Tarzan or the dauntless Doctor Livingstone. Born in the dying years of the empire, in one of its West Indian islands; then growing up in this former imperial capital, I innocently imbibed the fabrications and myths surrounding Africa.

During those years of innocence I was vaguely aware of the Africans living in my neighbourhood. They were mostly Nigerians (Yorubas) who had come to Britain as students but distracted by filial responsibilities, debts, love, boredom, failure, abandoned their studies for jobs with London Transport, British Rail or The Post Office. They resembled us 'West Indians' (as we called ourselves then) physically but had their own language, unusual names, and on warm weekend days dressed in colourful voluminous clothes that no respectable West Indian would be seen dead in. Occasionally, West Indian and African would exchange insults that carried a far more bitter sting than the imprecations that West Indians from different islands often hurled at each other. It was a neighbourhood of immigrants, strangers to these shores; strangers to themselves.

Suddenly, the comic books, boys' adventure stories and film versions of Africa were violently challenged, when, estranged from the White culture in which I lived, I embarked on an adolescent voyage of cultural self-discovery. Certain writers, poets and political activists and movements served as guiding lights: the Black Power Movement in the United States; Rastafarianism; Malcolm X, Marcus Garvey, Claude McKay, and C. L. R. James. All in different ways proffered radically new ways of seeing Africa, which exposed the seemingly innocuous comic-book and film images of my childhood as something poisonous, their consumption a form of not only cultural but also spiritual self-degradation. Mine was not a new discovery, nor was I alone in making it: Rastafarianism gave a whole generation a view of Africa as a source of cultural redemption. While some members of the preceding generation had discovered Africa through the Afro-hairstyle and dashiki shirt, a much larger number among my generation found it in reggae songs like Peter Tosh's 'African', which has the lyrics: 'No matter where you come from, as long as you are a black man, you're an African'. Rastafarianism has long since lost its influence, but Africa as cultural symbol – which predated that movement – survives. Amongst militant rap musicians, medallions in the shape of the African continent are *de rigueur*. Perhaps every generation of African descendants in the West is destined to pay renewed homage to the spirit of Africa.

My perception of Africa changed yet again when – at the age of twenty-four – I took up an appointment in a northern Nigerian university. I stayed for two eventful years. During that time I experienced too many everyday frustrations, saw too much poverty and disease, and heard too many stories of corruption and political chicanery to continue viewing Africa solely through the dewy eyes of a young man in search of his roots. Deciding against an academic career, I returned to Britain and entered journalism. The African continent, however, continued to exert a powerful fascination and I soon became a dispassionate chronicler of its coups, civil wars, famines and droughts. From an Africa of White fantasies to Africa as a source of cultural identity to an Africa of political turmoil and human tragedy: so my perceptions have changed.

This book is in part a personal account of my experience of travelling through West Africa in 1990 for the purpose of making a radio series. It is also an idiosyncratic report on some aspects of contemporary politics and culture in that region. The Africa of cities provides its backdrop, with the exception of a brief, but important, foray into the Cameroonian countryside.

The title of the book is derived from its early focus on two countries created for and by African descendants who returned to the continent from the New World – Sierra Leone and Liberia. It explores how these repatriate Africans and their descendants fitted into African society, and the kind of political and cultural relationship they established with indigenous Africans. The impact of 'New World Africans' is a recurrent, though by no means exclusive theme. It was for me as well, of course, a return to Africa.

The journey was made for BBC Radio Four. Thanks to Noah Richler, the producer, for his hard work, endurance, and dogged persistence in finding interviewees as we travelled.

Thanks also to Cameron Duodu, Alfred Zack-Williams, Kaye Whiteman of *West Africa* magazine and Tom McKaskie of the Centre for West African Studies for their contacts.

Special thanks to all those people who agreed to talk, sometimes at considerable risk to their safety. They include, Bishop George Brown of the Episcopalian Church, Kenneth Best, Ephraim John, Elaine and Eddie Dunn (for their hospitality, too), Portus Diallou, Cheikh Hamidou Kane, Fatou Sow, Abdullahi Bathally, Eyo and Butake, Wole Soyinka, Dora Chidzea, Doyin Abiola, Adu Boahen, Kwame Ahin, and Efua Sutherland-Addy.

I am especially grateful to Tunde Obadina and Ayesha Imam for their original invitation, in 1979, to visit Africa and for their stimulating conversations on African affairs over many years.

A very special thanks to Duncan Campbell for his unstinting encouragement, and to Alex O'Kunnor for the engaging hours of recreation he provided while I worked on the book.

Profound thanks also to Patrick Wilmot who read an early draft and made several invaluable suggestions for improvement. He is not, of course, responsible for my errors or oversights.

Finally, this book would not have been written without financial assistance from the Cadbury's Trust and the M. K. O. Abiola Foundation; thank you.

PRELUDE

On the way to Gatwick Airport, stuck in a traffic jam on Tower
Bridge, I suddenly became aware of the faint pulsations of a
curious nervousness. This was not the familiar traveller's anxiety about things that might have been forgotten, tasks left
unfinished, or the disastrous possibility of missing the plane.
My preparations for the journey had been reasonably thorough;
and included allowing ample time for crossing London on a damp
Friday evening. No, the uneasiness I felt was of an entirely
different order; vague, new, its causes untraceable. Eventually
my thoughts focused on the slight sore on my left arm, the
result of the many injections I'd received as protection against
the countless diseases in Africa. And I decided that I was in
danger of succumbing to an ailment that often afflicts travellers
to Africa: a fear of Africa.

I would later discover the real cause of that peculiar agitation.
But for now, seated in a mini-cab crawling fitfully across Tower
Bridge, I remembered my visit to a private clinic in Piccadilly.
Its recommended list of injections for prospective travellers to
the African continent would discourage all but the least faint-
hearted from ever visiting Africa – yellow fever, tetanus, polio,
typhoid, cholera and smallpox. The nurse who'd administered
the injections, simultaneously related tales of people who had
been struck ill in Africa, some mortally. I had listened to her
with the scepticism of one who had survived several trips
there without falling victim to a serious illness. Her cautionary
tales now made Sunday morning walks across a fog-bound
Hackney Marsh – an open space near where I lived – filled
with nothing more exciting than the hoarse exhortations of
league football players, appear the safest, most sensible way

to pass the winter. I resolved to relax, I spoke to the cab-driver.

He was an African, a slim, smooth-faced Yoruba and obviously new to the cab-driving business. He had asked me the route to Gatwick Airport and I had suggested that we cross the Thames at Tower Bridge. He seemed unperturbed by our slow pace; he sat languidly tapping his long thick index fingers on the steering-wheel in perfect rhythm to the beat of a soul tune on the radio. After a few minutes of talking I asked what had brought him to London.

'I'm a surveyor,' he said. 'I came to get better qualifications.'

'Couldn't you have got them in Nigeria?'

'Yes. But there was no work. Here I will get some more qualifications and work. When I go home, I can start my own business.'

'Doing what?'

'Anything. You know, in Nigeria today to survive you must be prepared to do anything. Only money matters and to get it you must do anything.'

'Anything?' I said.

'Anyyything ggg. Man must chop. See me. One degree in land surveying. No job. So one day I say to myself let me try this Western world of dreams. See me now. I drive a car. OK, OK, I have to drive a cab to own a car. But in Ibadan I didn't own a car and I couldn't drive a cab.'

'Why couldn't you drive a cab in Ibadan?'

'Me? I am graduate. I have a whole degree. It would have shamed my family.'

'But you're doing it here, driving a cab.'

'My family doesn't know. Every month I send some money home. Small, small. They appreciate it. Twenty pounds is over two hundred nairas.'

'Why didn't you try somewhere else in Africa, rather than coming all the way to London?'

He laughed sardonically and said: 'My friend, Africa is a mess. All over the continent. Our leaders betrayed us. Nigeria should be the richest country in Africa. But we have nothing. Our leaders have it all in Swiss bank accounts. When they have stolen enough money, they arrange a coup to give their friends a chance to chop. Then they come here and live like kings. One day I gave one small boy a ride. A Nigerian, but with one posh accent. He was at boarding school. I took him to Marble Arch. He gave me fifty pounds. Fifty pounds from a bag that he just, you know, dipped his hands in. I say to myself, his father chop well, well.'

'So what do you think of Britain?'

'You mean the racism?'

'No, just the country generally.'

'I'm dying to leave. When I first came I was applying for all sorts of jobs that wanted my qualifications. But I couldn't even get an interview. My degree doesn't count for anything here. I can clean offices, be a security guard, work in McDonald's, drive a cab. That's it.'

'Are you angry at the British people?'

'No. A white man is a white man. But I am angry at our leaders. They are the ones who are responsible. Shagari, Buhari, Babangida, Mobutu, Boigny, Doe and all those pretend leaders.'

'What's to be done about them?'

'They must go. Africa needs leaders who love their people. When you think of the crimes our leaders have committed. Too many.'

We talked at length about Africa's many ills, the droughts, coups, famine and South Africa. He told me a joke: a certain African president visiting a certain European country was presented with a fabulous piece of cloth intended for a suit. But for years this president could not find a tailor who could make a suit out of it. Tailors in Europe, America and Asia told him either that the cloth was too small for a suit, or he was too big. In the capital city of his own country he got a similar response. Finally, one day the president was visiting a remote village in his country. Passing a tailor's shop, he stopped to ask whether the tailor could make a suit from this cloth, which he had taken to travelling with wherever he went. The tailor accepted the assignment and the following day the president went to collect his suit. He was astonished to see the magnificent suit the tailor had made. 'How did you manage it?' the president asked in wonderment. 'Every tailor I have been to has said either the cloth is too small or I am too large'. 'With all respect, Mr President,' the tailor said, 'you see, in those places you were big. But here you are not big at all.'

*   *   *

The rear of the Boeing 747, stopping at Banjul, Freetown and Robertsfield, was filled with Africans. The stewardess's repeated messages forbidding passengers to smoke while standing were ignored by groups of men speaking loudly and excitedly in a Babel of languages. Here and there a few solemn Europeans, their tanned, dry faces betraying them as expatriates, sat with heads buried in magazines or newspapers.

I sat beside Noah, the producer with whom I was travelling. When we had met in the airport concourse Noah's anxiety had been palpable, but once seated he seemed at ease. We spent the first hour or so of the flight going over our schedule – six countries in two months. It was also an exercise in getting to know each other, as he had been assigned to the project about a month before because the original producer dropped out. I learnt then that he had spent three months travelling through Kenya. We exchanged notes on our experiences of that country.

After a while I felt a desperate need to stretch my legs. By the toilets I fell into conversation with four Africans. One was a majestically tall, slim sailor. He had the benign smile of people conscious of the potentially intimidating effect of their height and spoke with a soft voice. He was on his way back to The Gambia, having spent six months working on a Shell ship that travelled from the Gambian capital Banjul to Europe and then South America. His contract included a return fare home.

'The Senegambia federation is finished,' the tall African said. 'It was only a matter of time,' a scholarly looking young man said. He was a chemistry student, also Gambian. He went on to say that the Senegalese had tried to dominate the Gambians and failed to channel funds acquired in the federation's name to The Gambia.

'That's not the only reason,' the sailor said. 'They're Francophone and we are Anglophone. The two will never get on.'

'But you're all Africans,' I said. 'Why should you allow that colonial past to divide you?'

'That's just the way it is,' said the student. 'It's sad. But that's Africa.'

A third member of the party, a short, stocky fellow holding a half-bottle of duty-free whisky, in a tone of drunk aggression that matched a hard pugnacious face, said: 'Let the Francophones go. They are too arrogant.'

He proceeded to tell us about an altercation he had had with some Senegalese soldiers on his last visit to Banjul. (In 1981 Senegal rallied behind Sir Dawda Jawara's government during a coup attempt and Senegalese troops moved into Banjul. The coup attempt accelerated a process of unification that had been progressing at a seemingly reluctant pace.)

The short, stocky Gambian wandered off in search of ciga-rettes. I returned to my seat. Some minutes later he slumped down beside me.

'So you are Jamaican,' he said.

'In a fashion,' I said.

'My young brother. He is a Rastafarian.'

'In Banjul?'

'No. In Gothenburg, Sweden. It's not easy for me, having a brother who is a Rastafarian.' A drunken melancholy had replaced his earlier drunken aggression.

'Why?'

'Because of my work.'

'What work do you do?'

'You ask too many questions,' he said. He wandered off again. This time to get a fresh bottle of drink. When he returned he asked why I wanted to know what work he did. I said I was curious because he was embarrassed by his brother's faith or hairstyle. He moved closer, lowered his voice and said: 'I am a cop.'

'You're a cop in Sweden?'

'Oh, yes. Five years I have been a policeman in Sweden. My brother, he wants to study. So I send for him. Then he becomes a Rastafarian.'

'Is he still studying?'

'No. He does nothing. It's very difficult for me and my family.' He showed me a photograph of a plump blonde-haired woman and a cherubic brown child with a mop of curly hair. 'This is my wife and daughter,' he said. 'My wife, she is very beautiful, yes.'

I agreed without sincerity and asked why they were not travelling with him. He said his wife did not like Africa, that she kept on fainting when he brought her home on their honeymoon. 'Anyway,' he said, 'I am working. I am not going to The Gambia on holiday. I am working.'

'The Swedish police have sent you to Africa on an assignment,' I said.

'Maybe,' he said, revelling in my intrigue. 'I cannot discuss my work.'

He wandered off and we did not speak again. But he passed me several times before disembarking in Banjul. On each occasion he seemed drunker, and looked at me in a strange way, as if he regarded my Jamaicanness as proof of my complicity in the corruption of his impressionable younger brother – whom he had brought to Sweden from Africa to educate – with preposterous notions of Jah, and repatriation to an African Zion. With the absence of his bloodshot accusing eyes, the remainder of my flight passed more comfortably.

ONE

'DADDY, NO LOSE WE THIS COUNTRY'

Five years had passed since my last visit to Africa and there was much I had forgotten and had to relearn, and there were many new lessons to be absorbed in my first forty-eight hours.

Within an hour of landing at Robertsfield International Airport I found myself in a tiny windowless room. A female immigration officer sat behind a desk laboriously counting a wad of landing cards. Directly opposite me her male colleague was dozing, with his feet on the table. He intermittently awakened with a start, surveyed the room with a sleepy, red-eyed gaze, then sank into sleep again.

Somewhere in the building Noah was searching for a telephone to call our host, Kenneth Best, the editor of *The Observer*, then the only independent newspaper in Liberia. The Liberian Embassy in London had failed to brief us on the procedures for journalists wishing to enter Liberia. Our host should have been here to meet us. Without his presence we would not be allowed to leave the airport.

There was a telephone in this airless room, an antiquated Bakelite instrument, which could only make internal calls. It could not call Monrovia, the Liberian capital, some twenty miles away.

For a while I found ironic amusement in the possibility that I, a Jamaican, a person of African ancestry, might be denied entry into a country that had been founded by freed slaves from

the United States and once attracted thousands of settlers of
African descent from the New World. I then began to imagine
all kinds of terrible scenarios of expulsion and imprisonment. I
urged myself to keep calm, be optimistic. I remembered arriving
in Maputo Airport at night and confronting the prospect of
spending an uncomfortable night on the gritty airport floor
because the Mozambican Ministry of Information had not
informed immigration and security of my arrival. That night,
five years ago, I had ended up between the crisp starched
sheets of a bed in the Polana Hotel. This memory comforted
and relaxed me. As did the knowledge that it was early morning:
our host should be found long before nightfall.

Nevertheless, confined in the closed, oppressive room with
the morning slowly ticking away, I was unable to remain calm for
long. Suddenly the cause of the curious agitation I had sensed on
the way to Gatwick became clear: I was proposing to travel
through Africa in the company of a White person. During the
months of preparation for the journey I had, of course, felt an
unmistakeable twinge of apprehension. I thought I had assuaged
it by reminding myself that I was a professional broadcaster, a
dispassionate chronicler who had long abandoned the emotional
view of Africa as a cultural symbol. As a detached observer I
could happily make the journey. However, as a Jamaican
brought up in London and who had discovered Africa through a
miasma of White lies, I baulked at the very idea of such a
journey. This extremely emotional perception of Africa now
swelled inside me. In its possession, I saw the producer as a
millstone around my neck, blamed him for my confinement,
convinced myself that if I had entered Liberia alone I would not
be suffering in this sweaty claustrophobic room. Expulsion and
a swift return to London now seemed like the best outcome of
an ill-conceived project.

While the female immigration officer ponderously counted the
landing cards and her dozy colleague slept fitfully, I fought a
silent battle to regain the equanimity with which I had started
the journey. The sudden entrance of a smartly dressed officer
helped. He seemed to enter the room on a warm breeze. His
uniform looked new and clean, unlike the faded shiny blue of

the others, and he was clean-shaven and wore reflector-lens sunglasses, which gave him a sinister appearance.

'I need some fresh air,' I said truculently.

The sleeping officer woke up with a start. On seeing his superior he snapped himself upright and adjusted his uniform. A superfluous act, as the uniform was irredeemably worn and misshapen.

'You can walk on the landing,' the smart officer said, and in a reproachful tone ordered his subordinate to accompany me. This also seemed superfluous: I was unlikely to flee the airport.

Still, I nodded gratefully and walked out on to the landing. It was much cooler than the room, and there was a view beyond the airport: a green wooden house surrounded by a broken fence; a big, sprawling mango tree, a circular patch of ochre-coloured earth beneath it. The cooler air and the view of an open space were soothing. I began to feel less hostile towards my absent companion, and soon a little contrite for my earlier unkind thoughts. Gradually I forced the vicious jinnee of apprehension back into the bottle.

Leaning against the wall, the brighter light on his face, the immigration officer looked younger than his grey hair had earlier suggested. At the most he was in his late thirties.

A young boy selling cigarettes, sweets and kola-nuts climbed the stairs. He stared at me with large, pleading eyes. I showed him my cigarettes. The guard, suddenly alert, called the boy and bought a kola-nut from him, parting with a smooth worn coin. The boy wandered back down the stairs and his rubber slippers made a flip, flop noise which echoed long after he had disappeared.

The kola-nut in the officer's hand was large and purplish, a sign that it would taste bitter. He snapped it in two and held out a piece to me. I was surprised by this gesture. I had been feeling like a captive and regarded him as my captor. But with this gesture, he further allayed the fears which had risen in the hot, gloomy room. I knew then we would be allowed to enter Liberia; there would be no turning back. I accepted the kola-nut of friendship.

The officer and I tried to communicate, but his English –

spoken in a nasal American drawl that was also recognisably African – was difficult to follow. I gathered that he had been to a party the previous night and had come straight to work. When his shift finished he planned to go home, sleep, and then find another party.

I complained that the London Embassy had not properly informed us on the procedures for entering his country. He chewed meditatively on the kola-nut before answering: 'De invashun, de big cheefs say make we tighten security.'

I surmised that the London Embassy had not been informed. The invasion that the officer referred to had been reported in the London papers. But those reports had given the impression that the insurgents had been routed. I had not in any case attached much significance to the news of the invasion because President Samuel Doe's government was annually threatened by a coup.

The officer's superior called him and I was left standing on the landing alone, chewing a bitter kola-nut of arrival.

By the time a successful Noah returned close to midday, I had resumed my mask of composure, enabling me to greet him without betraying any signs of the disquiet I had experienced during his absence. Soon a young lady bearing a letter from Kenneth Best arrived, securing our entry, and we were speeding along an undulating road towards Monrovia, where we booked into the Ducor Palace Hotel. I passed Saturday afternoon in my room and in the evening spent a few uneventful hours in the company of Noah and two Liberian journalists, Ephraim and Budu. I had not fully recovered from my traumatic entry into the country and so felt very marginal to the gathering. But I did notice Ephraim, whom I looked forward to meeting after I'd had a good night's sleep.

The following morning, as I made my way down to breakfast, I met an American-sounding lady in the elevator. The lift was creaky and its descent hesitant. Our eyes met in shared uncertainty. Would we touch down safely?

Walking away from the elevator, she casually remarked that she could remember the days when the Ducor Palace was the best hotel in West Africa. 'Those were the days when champagne flowed in Monrovia,' she said. She was middle-aged, copper-coloured and her accent was a strange mixture of Africa and educated East-Coast America. I guessed she was an Americo-Liberian but because I was new to the country I could not yet identify one with certainty.

Her tone had been so blasé I imagined that she had started drinking champagne with her mother's milk. Her Gucci handbag, loose purple linen dress, her dignified but relaxed comportment, her lightly powdered face – all strengthened the impression of belonging to a privileged class.

'I can't stand champagne,' I teased. 'The smallest drop gives me a terrible headache.'

'That's unfortunate for you,' she said coolly.

'*Touché*,' I said, and we both laughed.

We exchanged names while walking to the terrace, and sharing the same breakfast table there seemed as natural as sharing the elevator. There was a serene quality about the morning which made me feel disinclined to start asking questions of the world. But this supremely self-assured lady aroused my professional curiosity. The 1980 coup that brought Master-Sergeant Samuel Doe to power was reportedly fuelled by native resentment of the Americo-Liberian élite who ran the country. The radio programme I had in mind would relate the fascinating history of Liberia as one example of how African descendants in the West attempted to recolonise a part of Africa. This Americo-Liberian lady seemed to present an unmissable opportunity to start my research.

We talked for some time about inconsequential matters, then the conversation suddenly became serious when she asked if I was related to the Dennises of Liberia.

'Not as far as I know. I am a Jamaican,' I replied.

'I am always surprised at how people from the islands assert their origins. So much pride. I used to be proud to call myself a Liberian.'

'Before the champagne stopped flowing,' I said.

She smiled fleetingly, then her expression changed, became embittered, mocking. 'Before these buffoons took over,' she said. 'The Master-Sergeant.'

'From the little I know of your country's history, Americo-Liberians brought it upon yourselves,' I said.

'My dear, we brought progress and order to this country. The Master-Sergeant and his cronies have destroyed that.'

'They would call it a revolution.'

'They shot people on the beaches. Called it an execution. They shot people's husbands, brothers, uncles, fathers. They shot them in cold blood sometimes, or they held mock trials; then shot them. Killed them on the beaches.'

'That, sadly, is the way of revolutions. It claims lives,' I said without conviction. 'But the Master-Sergeant must enjoy some popularity; he has been able to stay in power for a decade.'

'Do you know how many coup attempts have been made against him in those ten years?'

I shook my head, though I knew that Doe's regime was extremely unstable.

'At least ten. That's one each year.'

'I am sure some were figments of his imagination.'

'Possibly. But most were not. When I lived in Monrovia, I used to employ people. And let me tell you, I had to give careful thought to who I employed, which tribe they came from. Because some tribes simply did not get on with each other.'

'That sounds, to me, dangerously similar to those White South Africans who argue that without their presence the Africans there would be at each other's throats.'

'I don't know about South Africa,' she said firmly. 'But Liberia I do know about. We created harmony amongst the tribes. The Master-Sergeant has destroyed that.'

'I don't exactly see Africans killing each other on the streets of Monrovia,' I said.

'Not yet. Not yet,' she said ominously.

This line of conversation ended when the waiter brought our breakfast. As we ate, she asked what I was doing in Liberia. When I told her that I was a journalist on an assignment, she visibly blushed, as if moments before she had been indiscreet. Our breakfast together ended shortly after that. (When I next saw her, the following day, in the hotel lobby, we spoke briefly and she expressed such concern that I might use her name that I gave her my word that I wouldn't.)

Later that same morning Noah and I had our first proper conference since arriving. He wore a fretful expression that I had seen on other radio producers before they had made their first recording on a foreign assignment. This was reflected in his schedule for the working week in Monrovia. It was solidly packed with actual or potential interviews, and, most worrying, failed to take account of the afternoon heat. I advised that we tried to avoid moving about for the first few hours of the afternoon or we would soon exhaust ourselves. But what was to me a commonsensical observation was met with a sort of petulant resentment, which made me conscious of the differences in our age. I was about five years older than him.

Noah reminded me that he had travelled around East Africa and I reminded him that we were in an entirely different part of the continent. During this exchange my earlier misgivings resurfaced, but this time they were accompanied by an incipient awareness of having returned to Africa in the company of an inexperienced producer who would drag me through West Africa like a piece of recording machinery, if I was not careful.

Somehow we managed to thrash out the schedule and moved on to the contents of the programme. Conversations held the previous day had convinced me that we might have to revise the original focus of this first programme – the history of the Americo-Liberians. Somewhere in the north of Liberia, despite government propaganda to the contrary, government troops were still locked in battle with an army of insurgents. Should we try to visit the battle zone? How would the invasion fit into our focus on the Americo-Liberians? These were questions for me to answer as the content of the series was my responsibility.

The person I hoped would help us to answer these and other questions, or direct us to people who could, was Ephraim John, the journalist I had met the previous evening, who worked for *The Observer*. I had found him engaging. Over great quantities of beer this impish reporter with a charmingly mischievous smile had admitted to being a failed pop-musician, and a reformed

alcoholic prone to occasional lapses; a sin for which he atoned
by playing the organ at a Baptist church. His editor and our host,
Kenneth Best, belonged to the same church and had invited us
to attend Sunday worship. Ephraim would take us there.

Ephraim arrived late and groggy from a hangover – he'd drunk
most of the beer – which he assured me would be cured by a
penitential session at the organ. Indeed, he implied that his
performance would be all the better for it. He also suggested
it would be politic if we made a courtesy call on the Minister of
Information. That it was a Sunday did not matter as he and the
Minister were tribesmen (Bassa) and sometimes drank
together. How fortunate, I thought, we were to have a guide
as well-connected as Ephraim.

With this new item on the day's agenda we drove off on our
first day's work. It was mid-morning now and Monrovia's main
thoroughfare, Broad Street, was almost deserted. Only a few
battered orange-coloured taxis plied it. The city was still
recovering from its Saturday-night revelry.

Suddenly, we had reached the Minister's house and were
piling out of the car. Ephraim marched ahead with an urgent,
self-important swagger. Noah followed carrying his tape
recorder and I lagged behind, feeling somewhat stunned by this
abrupt change of pace. I caught up with the others in a room at
the top of a flight of stairs. Ephraim stood before a timid-looking
young girl – a servant? – and she pointed down a corridor. Then
Ephraim marched off again and we duly followed. I was the last
to enter a spacious room lined with armchairs and settees most
of which were occupied. In a central position sat an immense
African man wrapped in a dressing-gown, his face lit up in surprise. He was flanked by a portly white-haired Lebanese and a
middle-aged African lady; they were equally surprised. Ephraim's bearing changed as he approached the man, became
humble. Before I could get a proper measure of the situation I
heard Noah say: 'I'll handle this.' Ephraim had by now shaken
the Minister's hand, said something, was retreating. Noah
stepped forward and with a stutter introduced himself. I
remained in the background expecting to be introduced, but
sensing that we were in the middle of a diplomatic disaster.

Noah's words were too low and disjointed; his nerves consumed him. His knees trembled along with his hesitant voice.

Embarrassed by his performance, I stepped forward, introduced myself to the Minister and, as lucidly as I could, explained the purpose of our visit to Liberia. I tried to keep a smile on my face, to convey that I found the situation as embarrassing as he did.

He heard me out, nodded, and a mischievous smile crossed his lips. Then he switched his attention to Noah, saying 'You', in a deep, bassy voice; emphatic and authoritative. I retreated to the background, feeling as though I'd been dismissed, that the Minister saw better game in the young White man. He was clearly enjoying this encounter: watched by the admiring members of his court he had reduced a White man to a ball of nerves, reversing what seemed like the natural order of the world.

Noah resumed with greater composure and even managed to elicit a more respectful smile from the Minister, who assured him that the Ministry would provide whatever assistance was necessary to make our programme. But by now I was stewing with humiliation.

When the Minister had finished with us, I stormed back to the car. There, I called Noah aside and severely admonished him for his incompetence in putting me in such a humiliating position. But he refused to acknowledge that a disaster had occurred or that he was in any way responsible. We argued bitterly. When I threatened to handle all meetings with officials myself – to avoid further humiliation – he finally admitted that the encounter with the Minister could have been better conducted.

We drove on to church, the car weighed down by a strained silence. Once again shrill alarm bells of regret for having begun this journey rang loudly in my head. But it was far too late for those bells. Somehow, for both our sakes and the project's, I would have to stifle my misgivings and find a tactful way of restraining my callow, youthful White companion.

The church was in Crozerville, a village outside Monrovia that had been settled by Barbadians. A centennial memorial at the village entrance reads: '1865–1965, This monument is erected to the Sacred Memory of the immigrants from Barbados in the West Indies who landed near this spot (Receptacle Creek), May 10, 1865'.

By the time we reached Crozerville Baptist church, I was less upset but remained pensive. And somewhere in the back of my mind was a growing intrigue with the severity of my own reaction to the incident in the Minister's house. Entering the church I forgot about the morning's mishap for the time being.

It was a small wooden church and a warm dry breeze blew through open windows. A plump pastor delivered an uninspiring sermon in a thick, almost incomprehensible American accent. The choir sang lustily and exultantly. Looking around at the congregation I was struck by the familiarity of the scene. The women in flowery nylon dresses, some wearing flamboyant hats; the men in ill-fitting suits; boys in too-large or too-small suits but wearing them all the same with great aplomb; girls with their hair plaited and tied with colourful ribbons – I could have been at a church in Jamaica.

After the service we were introduced to several elderly sons and daughters of Crozerville. When they heard of my Jamaican connection, they proudly revealed their own New World links. Mrs Brown's grandmother came from Barbados, Mr Stewart's grandfather from South Carolina, Mrs Harris's great-grandfather from Jamaica, her grandmother from Virginia. And you must meet Mr MacDonald, his father came from Boston and fought in the First World War. Then we ate lunch of fried chicken and fish in the church hall; and the food, like the service, tasted of the Caribbean. It was served, with sugary-sweet soft drinks, by a group of middle-aged ladies who organised the children and men with military precision and amid much laughter and offers of second helpings.

Afterwards we drove back to Kenneth Best's house. His wife ran a bakery from their home, and she served up a Sunday dinner – more fish and fowl – which climaxed with home-baked tarts and home-made ice-cream. In the cool, deep-walled living-room – which succeeded in looking both bare and lived in – laden

and leadened with two meals of hospitality, the Sunday afternoon took on a hazy, somnolent character.

When the post-lunch torpor passed, we, inevitably, started
talking about Liberian politics. Mr Best saw worrying signs in
the invasion, the insurgents had reportedly entered the country
through the Ivory Coast. Speculation was rife that the Ivorien
government was involved.

As he spoke, Mr Best's frustration and disappointment with
the course of his country's politics emerged: 'In 1980,' said
Best, 'Liberia was at peace with all her neighbours. All. Today
the finger-pointing tells you we're not. In 1980 most of the
tribes were basically together – the only problem was the
leadership.

'I urged the government, Mr Tolbert at the time, to overhaul
the electoral system and put into the hands of the people the
decision-making for the choice of the leaders and for the major
policies that affect their destiny. And I said that if Mr Tolbert
did that he would go down in history as one of Africa's great
leaders because you are dealing with a continent where you
have scores of life presidents, military dictators and people who
just perpetuate themselves in power by rigging the ballot. They
didn't take it seriously.

'Africa's problem and Liberia's too,' he said with conviction,
'is that it has failed democracy.'

Best used the term 'revolution' in describing the 1980 coup
which ousted the Tolbert government, ending over a century of
Americo-Liberian dominance. But he suggested that the divide
between natives and Americo-Liberians had been exaggerated.
Few Americo-Liberians, he averred, had no blood links with the
natives. In the household of his childhood, the term 'up-country'
people – the tribes of the interior – was banned, because his
mother considered it pejorative.

The hospitality of the Crozerville congregation and the Bests
seemed to repair the rift between Noah and me. We departed
the Bests' home in a convivial mood and, with Ephraim, spent
the remainder of the afternoon on the beach.

On the way back to Monrovia, we stopped at the National
Cultural Village, a community of artists – sculptors, actors,

musicians and painters. In a crowded auditorium we watched a play about juju and Christianity, a modern morality tale, which to judge from the audience's laughter, touched a popular chord. Later we passed two soldiers in the car park; they were tall and lean and mean-looking in their battle fatigues. Seeing my pale companion, they shouted: 'Welcome to Liberia. Everything is normal.' Reason enough to think the very opposite, I thought.

That night the ocean was quiet and waves of darkness stirred above it. Down below Mamba Point, the location of the hotel, lights shone in a seafront settlement, from which also trailed the smell of roasting fish and meat and yam and hot palm oil.

Looking out into this night from the balcony of my hotel room, nearing the end of my first forty-eight hours back in Africa, I began to suspect that I had arrived in a city whose outward calm concealed fears of an imminent upheaval in a nation yet to recover from an earlier bloody political transition. The mainly historical programme I had planned for Liberia now seemed less urgent, although not entirely irrelevant for understanding the particular cause of Liberia's current instability.

*   *   *

William R. Tolbert Jr., the eighteenth president of the Republic of Liberia, planned a life of idyllic retirement near his village on the outskirts of Monrovia. He was staying there one night in April 1980 when armed soldiers burst into his bedroom and dragged him out of bed. The shocked, sleepy President shouted for his guards but they did not respond. The soldiers ordered him to dress; they would drive him to formally hand over power to the new President. Somewhere between the President's retirement home and the Presidential residence in Monrovia, somewhere in that terrible night, perhaps drunk on fear, or inspired by the spirit of vengeance, the soldiers shot President William Tolbert Jr.

We visited President Tolbert's retirement home. It stands

on the ridge of a low-lying hill in Bensonville, at the end of a short drive along an immaculate road that passes through a grove of eucalyptus trees, which obscure wooden houses. Emerging from the sepulchral light of the grove, the road rises gently and on the summit is a vast glassy bronze cube, illuminated by the sunlight. Surrounded by wilderness, it strikes the eye like the creation of some inconceivably advanced civilisation.

But access to it was not easy. The ten-foot-tall wrought-iron gates were reached via a concrete path that was being reclaimed by the bush. We knocked and blew the car horn for some minutes before a mad-looking fellow appeared. He wore half-length khaki pants, revealing spindly legs and a torn, dirty stringed singlet and swung a machete as though it were an extension of his hand. He ordered us round to a side entrance and after Ephraim had spoken to him, allowed us entry.

He was an old soldier and he lived in the servants' quarters of the building. The grounds had become his farm. There he kept fowls and used the flower beds that fronted the house to grow sweet potatoes and peas. Stagnant green opaque water filled a fountain bowl.

The house has no windows. It had been fitted with a central air-conditioning unit that would maintain a constant temperature all the year round. Its doors were locked and the old soldier guarded the grounds. He did not know who had the keys, nobody ever used the house. It simply stood there in a semi-wilderness, a folly, a monument to a dream that ended as a nightmare.

President William R. Tolbert's retirement home is one of many monuments in and around Monrovia to what started out as an extraordinary chapter in the history of West Africa, and ended up following the same pattern of post-independence politics as the rest of the region: coups, attempted coups, counter-coups.

For over a century Liberia was the only independent West African state. Its first president, J. J. Roberts, is remembered by a discoloured, decaying statue of a tall, grim-looking man in a stovepipe hat and tail-coat, which stands near the Ducor Palace

Hotel. At the base of the statue is a frieze depicting the landing, in 1822, of freed African-American slaves who had been given a free passage back to Africa. The frieze also shows the battles with local chiefs, the signing of peace treaties; and finally the raising of the flag in 1847 to declare the birth of the Republic of Liberia. Roberts' statue looks down on to the Masonic Temple on Cape Mesurado. A massive red-brick structure topped with the Freemason's globe, the building is now disused. Its windows are boarded up, its giant Gothic gates chained together.

Decades after the founding of the Republic the settlers remained on the coast and only the bravest ventured into the hinterland, up country. Benjamin Anderson was among the first. Born in Baltimore, Maryland, he journeyed to the hinterland between 1868–9 and again in 1874. *Narrative of a Journey to Musardu* (published in 1874) chronicles his adventures.

Anderson ignored constant rumours of inter-tribal warfare up country and travelled to Musardu with a view to making friendly contact with natives and opening trade routes for the young colony. But his passage was often obstructed by chiefs who he described as 'barbarians'. One such was King Bessa, who detained Anderson in his town, and encouraged a revolt amongst the explorer's Congo bearers. Anderson writes:

'Bessa, in carrying out this policy of non-intercourse with the interior, which is a standing well known, and agreed upon thing through the whole country, now commenced a series of annoyances, his people acting in concert with him. He began with the Congoes. Every means that language and signs could produce was used to frighten and discourage them. They were told of the wars in the path . . . He then brought in his war drums, the heads of which were the skins of human beings, well tanned and corded down, while a dozen grinning human jaw bones were dangling and rattling against each other with a noise that reminded my Congoes that their jaws too might perform a similar function.'

Anderson's Congoes were reduced to pleading with him to turn back, saying 'Daddy, no lose we this country, no lose we.' The King encouraged these entreaties, advising the Congoes,

'Your Daddy has got the heart of an elephant; you had better talk to him.'

Not all the hinterland rulers were as belligerent as King Bessa. Some welcomed the military protection accompanying the expansion of the Liberian state, which was hastened by Europe's 'scramble for Africa' in 1885 and continued into the early years of the twentieth century. Despite the incorporation of seventeen tribes, the Liberian state remained firmly controlled by the Americo-Liberian minority. Paradoxically, Liberia became a refuge for political exiles from colonial governments elsewhere on the African continent in the 1940s and 1950s, while a small élite perpetuated Americo-Liberian ascendancy through rigged elections, a weak legislature, and continual frustration of the aspirations of native Liberian politicians. Uppity native politicians were sometimes reminded just what they owed the Americo-Liberians. As President Tubman – generally considered a liberal – felt it necessary to do in 1951 in an address directed at a native politician:

'Let it be remembered that when those great men and women first landed here from the United States to found this nation, they met not a single solitary one of their brothers who were civilised and educated, nor were the traces of Christian religion anywhere seen or known.'

With William R. Tolbert's death Americo-Liberian dominance ended. The new government was no less susceptible to ethnic rule but it recognised the strength of feelings amongst native Liberians against what was perceived as a colonial government, albeit one which was not European.

Destroying the symbols of Americo-Liberian rule helped to legitimise the coup and enhance the government's popularity. One of the first symbols destroyed was a statue to Matilda Newport. Among the early battles between settlers and natives, Matilda Newport, a schoolteacher born in Philadelphia, purportedly fired a cannon which repulsed the army of an attacking tribe, the Dukors. She became immortalised as a national hero and an annual public holiday was held in her name. But indigenous Liberians regarded Matilda Newport and the

celebrations surrounding her as a symbol of all that was wrong
with the nation before 'the revolution'.

Some native Liberians referred to events like Matilda
Newport Day in such resentful, indignant tones, that I was
occasionally left with the impression of being in a nation recently
emerged from colonialism, rather than West Africa's oldest independent state. These feelings were calmly summed up to me
by a Liberian political scientist, Joseph Guannu: 'Some Liberians
could never have joyously celebrated Matilda Newport Day
because it reopened the wounds inflicted in the battles of 1822
. . . the holiday served the interest of only one group.'

In spite of the poor relations between natives and settlers
Liberia long remained the promised land to many poor, alienated
African descendants who could see no future in the USA and
the Caribbean. Although the majority of Americo-Liberians
arrived in the last century, some came this century.

One of the most successful of the recent arrivals was Clifford
Flemister, the Vice-President of Rovia Bank. He was born in
Tennessee, and came to Liberia in 1951. A powerfully built
man, his dashiki and rhetorical flourishes reminded me of radical
African-American political activists of the sixties. The kind of
person who, as Langston Hughes once said, would 'work to
make sure the doors are open wide and tell White folks like it
is so there's nowhere to hide'.

Interviewing him in his office, I was reminded of the strength
of the strange emotion which brought people back to Africa. Once
in our conversation, he became carried away, stood up, pulled at
his dashiki shirt and said: 'See this dashiki, I have worn it to meet
presidents, to meet *presidents*. I don't care; that's my roots.

'One of the first songs that my brother and I learnt when we
were growing up in Chicago was the Liberian national anthem.
My daddy was fond of recalling a story about when we were
born, my twin brother and me. A doctor picked one of us up
and said: "This young man may grow up to become President
of the United States one day." My father said, "Very unlikely
but I'll take them to a country where that may happen." So
coming to Liberia was something that was ingrained in us from
childhood.'

Flemister described his father as a devout follower of Marcus
Garvey, the Jamaican-born visionary who founded an organisation – the Universal Negro Improvement Association – which
flourished in the United States in the 1920s. Among Garvey's
numerous ambitious plans was the voluntary repatriation of Africans back to Africa. The organisation signed a deal with the
Liberian government to purchase an immense tract of land for
that purpose. But the government under President King
reneged on the deal and later sold the land to the Firestone
Rubber Company.

The Liberian banker was intimately familiar with this strange
and disgraceful episode in Liberian history. He recalled listening
to a conversation between his father and former President King
during which the Garvey incident was raised: 'My father and I
were sitting with the old man, and my father asked him how he
felt about it now. He said it was his single greatest mistake.
And tears rolled down my father's cheeks.'

Like many other Americo-Liberians, Flemister denied that
native resentment of Americo-Liberian rule had fuelled the 1980
coup. 'By 1980,' he argued, 'the issue had become moot. I think
I am one of the very few pure Americo-Liberians. By 1980 most
Americo-Liberians had become mixed, a quarter, or half. Even
those from the large great families were mixed. But some
people seized upon it. The issue was blown up out of proportion
by certain interest groups.'

Typically, the interview with Flemister about Liberia's recent
and distant past touched on the history being made as we spoke:
the invasion. It had been dominating the newspapers since my
arrival. Presidents Momoh of Sierra Leone and Conté of Guinea
had visited Liberia to reaffirm their commitment to a non-
aggression pact signed years before. Their visit had brought
traffic in Monrovia to a standstill. President Doe had days before
declared the Mandingoes of Nimba county – the scene of the
invasion – an inextricable part of Liberia and appealed to their
sense of patriotism. And on the day I met Flemister, the Liberian *Observer* reported – quoting the Liberian Chief of Army
Staff – that the invaders had been routed.

Flemister obviously prided himself on his gruff candour. He

was a man devoid of any romantic illusions about Africa and said
so forcefully. But he tactfully refrained from passing judgement
on Doe's ten-year rule. After all he was a banker, and his bank
appeared to be thriving. 'Nobody wants the invasion,' Flemister
said simply. 'People are fed up with all this killing and if we are
not careful we'll create another Uganda.'

This portentous comparison triggered my own memories of
Uganda – the war, my moments of fright; a new experience of
Africa. I was there in 1985, in Kampala, a city disintegrating
following a long period of instability caused, in part, by ethnic
rivalry. The insurgent force led by Yoweri Museveni, sub-
sequently the President of Uganda, was at the time of my visit
closing in on the capital. Government troops had lost all disci-
pline; robbing traders and looting property. In one frightening
incident, a nervous young teenage soldier pointed a Kalashnikov
in my face and demanded to see my papers. The hotel I stayed
in was daily robbed by drunken government soldiers. And a
Nigerian diplomat, with the coolness of a veteran, had compared
the unfolding drama to his country's own earlier civil war.
'These people are twenty years behind us,' he had said, implying
that a bloody civil war would teach ethnic chauvinists a salutary
lesson in nation building.

Before visiting Kampala, I enjoyed being able to move
amongst Africans without arousing the curious stares which my
role as stranger in Britain elicited. Even within London, the city
of my youth, people gaped at me, yet thousands of miles away,
amongst people whose language and customs I did not share,
my daily passage went unnoticed. An illusion, perhaps, but it
made me feel less the perpetual stranger. In the embattled
Ugandan capital this chameleonic asset no longer seemed advan-
tageous. There were times when I feared that my foreignness
and impartiality would not be recognised, that drunken, maraud-
ing soldiers might mistake me for a Ugandan. Flemister's fore-
boding reference to Uganda therefore triggered a mild panic in
me. Several people had already mistaken me for a Liberian; in
one instance, a relative. I was suddenly alert to the danger of
being trapped in a war-torn Monrovia, and from that moment
decided to constantly carry my passport, a British passport.

The irony of invoking my Britishness to survive the potential anarchy of Africa was not lost on me.

As we drove back to the hotel after speaking to Clifford Flemister, we got caught up in a traffic jam caused by a truckload of soldiers. Their vehicle, parked on the corner of a major junction, was causing an obstruction. They laughed and swore at protesting drivers, waving their weapons in the air like children playing with toy guns.

*   *   *

At the north end of Haile Selassie Drive is the main bridge across the Mesurado River. On weekday evenings, Monrovian workers pour across it towards Via Town and beyond. Reggae and soul, from nearby record shacks, combine with the shrill sound of car horns to create a cacophonous music. On the south bank of the Mesurado, smoke and voices and more music issue from buildings erected, it seemed to me, with a total disregard for the aesthetics of urban architecture. The Liberian flag, limp in the humid, windless air, stands atop a pole that rises from the dark, stagnant, fetid water which surrounds Providence Island.

It was here on Providence Island that the first shipload of African-Americans landed, the dream of returning to Africa finally a reality. The purported exact spot is marked by an immense cotton tree whose enormous buttresses create a great chamber where people could congregate, its branches and trunk draped with creepers. It is an eerie sight, the cotton tree. In Jamaica, as in most parts of West Africa, this tree is associated with the supernatural, regarded as a place to commune with the spirits and shown great reverence.

I was accompanied on my walk around the island by the Most Reverend George D. Brown, Bishop of the Anglican Church of Liberia and Archbishop of the Church of the Province of West Africa. The Bishop and I were on the island to talk about Liberian history, where the settlers had gone wrong.

The Liberian national motto was, until the revolution, 'The Love of Liberty brought us here'. This motto not only caused offence to the majority of Liberians, who had never left the African soil, it was also a half-truth. The early settlers had other motives. Their return journey had been funded by the American Colonisation Society – founded by White Christians influenced by the Sierra Leone experiment of 1787 – and they were regarded by their patrons, and regarded themselves, as Christian missionaries. They had come to spread the gospel, civilise the natives. Like their European counterparts, the Black missionaries disparaged native religions and viewed Africa as the 'dark continent' on which they would shine the light of Christianity.

'As elsewhere in Africa,' Bishop Brown explained, 'they thought before we could be civilised we had to change our name. My name is Kwafley. I am from a small tribe called the Grebo. All my indigenous people know me by the name Kwafley. Kwa means hand, fley, empty. But at that time they thought God could not or would not accept the name Kwafley. He had to accept George. They came to civilise.'

Missionaries in Liberia, and generally, the Bishop suggested, had a rather absurd view of religion. '. . . the missionaries thought that Christianity was the only way through which God revealed himself to man. This is typical of Western civilisation, the view that Christianity is the only true revelation that God has given to man. Anything that had to do with non-Christian religion was an anathema. So you couldn't use the drums, you couldn't even wear your clothes. You had to wear Western clothes.'

The Bishop made the last point in a tone of incredulity. 'We now know of course that you cannot say that God does not love a person because he does not have a Christian name.'

All modern Liberian churches are now headed by Liberians, Bishop Brown explained, and Christianity has incorporated certain concepts from local African religions. For example, '. . . the whole concept of the dead. For us death is home-going. So after you bury a person the next thing is a real feast. Not too much mourning. We say that because my father cared for me in this life, now that he is in the spirit world he is in a better position to care for me. There is a place in Christianity for this.'

I recalled to the Bishop my lunch with a senior Liberian journalist earlier that day. Before eating he crossed himself and whispered a brief prayer. We were about the same age and I could not imagine any of my British contemporaries, godless children of the post-modern age, enacting a similar ritual. So I asked Bishop Brown whether religion was more important to Africans than to Europeans.

'Yes, in Africa,' he said delightedly, straightening up as though tickled by the question, 'what we are and what we do is governed by a god. You can say it is because we have not yet developed the technology you have developed.

'. . . if I drive home safely tonight it is because God has been with me. You will say it is because of the condition of the road and the carefulness of the driver and all of that. For a typical African – and I don't mean those people who say they are African but do what they see other people do – there is no difference between the spiritual and the physical. We are because God is.'

However, Bishop Brown recognised a profound incompatibility between some aspects of African beliefs and Christianity. 'The African religion is basically a religion of fear. You don't trust people. Sin is not an offence to God. Sin is an offence to your neighbour when you are caught. It is a religion of fatalism. Faith is weak in traditional religion. It is also a religion of reprisal. So that word forgiveness is actually absent in African religions.'

I mentioned the play I'd seen at the Cultural Village on my first day in Liberia. A sick woman had gone to consult a medicine man, having given up on praying to God. The audience had laughed wildly. But Bishop Brown gave it a serious interpretation.

'The medicine man would say the only way I can help is to turn the medicine back upon the person who has touched you. Let the medicine affect the person the same way the person wants it to affect you. Vengeance. This is why Islam thrives.

Allah is just. He's merciful but he's just. And in as much as you have done this to me Allah has ordered me to take vengeance.'

The Bishop disagreed with the commonly held view that Liberia once had a caste system. The early settlers distinguished between aborigines, those untouched by Christianity, Liberians, those with religious teaching, and the Americo-Liberians. Mobility from one class to another was possible through education. 'My paternal grandfather was what you call a voodoo man. He was a witchdoctor. In our tribe he was what we call Bodiull. He was the custodian of the medicine of the tribe. My maternal grandfather was a priest in the Episcopal Church. Out of these two strange mixtures, I was able to evolve.'

Nevertheless, he admitted that there was a time when an Americo-Liberian surname opened doors to the corridors of privilege. Tolbert's demise was followed by ambiguous change and obdurate continuity: 'Some people call it a revolution. I call it a *coup d'état*. When President Doe got into power he tried to open the doors to all Liberians. But some people exploited that. They tried to reverse the order. They believed that now was the aborigines' time. Jobs were given on ethnic lines. What is needed is a blending of the two. For us to do it on the basis of merit. Not tribal connections. But the problem with our politicians is that because of the fear and fatalism in our culture, it is difficult . . .'

As we spoke, a convoy of soldiers were crossing the Mesurado Bridge, momentarily distracting me from listening to this urbane Liberian prelate, the offspring of a spiritual marriage between the Christianity of the settlers and native religious beliefs. The gods of politics and war, far less happy with the secular Americo-Liberian legacy, were abroad.

TWO

A NIGHT FOR NELSON MANDELA

We finished our last interview in Liberia on the cusp of a Friday evening. It took place in the Cultural Village, with its director, Flomo. Liberia's most popular comedian, he was skinny, phlegmatic; and his small bloodshot eyes were the most lively feature of a melancholy face.

The interview had not gone especially well. Flomo's talent served the revolution, mining the rich vein of comedy that lay in the clash between the old and the new in everyday life. Didactic comedy. I was disappointed, a little self-critical of my failure to extract more from him; but recognised that my disappointment owed much to my excessive – and ingenuous – expectations. A week in Liberia had exposed the tragedy of the Liberian experiment to me. It had also revealed the tragicomedy that followed: the lean, hungry, semi-literate soldier who seized power and became a bloated buffoon mimicking those he'd ousted by rigging elections, surrounding himself with his tribesmen. The comedy of an African revolution. From Flomo, a state official, I'd foolishly anticipated nuggets of subtle subversive humour.

Isaac Bantu, a freelance journalist, had arranged the interview and accompanied us. He was in fact far more interesting than Flomo, whom I suspected would have preferred a restful afternoon in preparation for that night's performance, rather than answering abstruse questions from two strangers, one sticking a microphone under his nose.

Flomo thrived partly because of the government: Bantu survived in spite of that same government. The most serious coup attempt against the Doe regime occurred in 1985, led by one of Doe's former comrades, Brigadier General Quinwonkpa. In the season of reprisal that ensued, Bantu was jailed and tortured to within an inch of his life. He counted himself lucky; hundreds were killed.

He refused to talk about his ordeal in detail but occasionally alluded to it. He once said: 'After Doe's jail, I fear nothing.' He was not boasting, this short, stocky, ferociously dignified Liberian. Merely stating a fact. I would later witness a minor but telling demonstration of his fearlessness. As we drove to his house one night we were stopped by a motorcycle policeman. Noah was driving and this was the second time he'd been stopped in as many days for allegedly breaking the lights. Noah had already contributed to the Policemen's Widows' Fund (a euphemism for a bribe). This time, with Bantu as a front-seat passenger, the fundraiser was disappointed. In response to the policeman's charge, Bantu gruffly retorted: 'Nonsense.' He demanded that we drive to the police station, where he 'Isaac Bantu' would speak to the officer's superior. The shocked policeman eventually rode away. An object lesson in handling official extortion.

That Friday evening, with the last Liberian interview taped, Bantu further impressed himself on my memory. He was inseparable from his Sony shortwave radio and every so often lovingly plucked it out of his bag to privately catch up on the latest world news. On this occasion he shared the news:

'They are going to release Nelson Mandela,' Bantu said.

We all crowded excitedly round the radio, the better to hear. It was true: the imprisoned human symbol of Black South Africa's liberation struggle, of Africa's independence aspirations, of Africans' long, long battle against White oppression; a man whose lengthy incarceration filled the hearts of Africans everywhere with a quiet, unspeakable shame but who continued living, keeping hope alive; Nelson Mandela could at last cry freedom. Incredible, wonderful news. Bantu, Flomo and I shook hands in spontaneous celebration.

On the long walk back to the car, the elation subsiding, Bantu observed drily: 'Maybe now we can think about the rest of Africa.' A poignant truth: Africa's prisons are filled with political prisoners, while African leaders condemn apartheid, distracting attention from their own domestic repression.

When we were alone, Noah, who had quietly observed the excitement between Flomo, Bantu and myself, reminded me that Mandela's release meant something to him, too. 'We should shake hands, too,' he said in a rather wounded tone of voice. 'It's a victory for our generation as well.' I felt humbled because I'd momentarily forgotten that as members of the same generation in the West, we had grown up in a world which, less marked by the sharp racial divisions of the past, allowed us common heroes and common causes. We warmly shook hands, as comrades; though not as friends.

Our relationship had improved during the course of the week. There had been no repeat of Sunday's embarrassing incident. Only a minor disagreement when I tactfully suggested he drop his habit of calling Africans 'Pal', because it sounded, to me, so superior and condescending; however different he intended the effect. He'd protested, naturally. But over a long, hard, sometimes fraught week, we'd taped hours of interviews. We were due to leave Liberia by road the following day. And Mandela would soon walk free. So, forgetting our squabbles, we decided to make our last night in Monrovia a night for Nelson Mandela.

Hence our visit to the surreal El Dorado pool hall. Here, a dense mist of chalkdust, warm, humid and laced with the odour of sweat, filled the air. The chalkdust – used to keep the players' hands dry – obscured silent players and spectators. The games were played on four chalk-laden tables, their whitish green surface aglow from the light of low-hanging shaded bulbs. The players stepped from the impenetrable mist, into the pools of light, crouched, aimed, shot; then were swallowed by the fog again. There was no talking, no laughter, just the sound of shuffling feet on the dusty floor, the dull echo of the balls kissing. It was unlike any pool hall I'd ever seen. Our presence stirred curiosity, like that of two strangers who'd just ridden into town. Our skills were tested by a slim, hungry-looking pool-hall hustler dressed in a black cowboy hat, denim shirt and jeans and pointed leather boots. We lost ten dollars between us. I sought consolation in the sentiment that when visiting, a wise man should allow his host the first victory in any game.

From the El Dorado we moseyed on down to a bar with a name similarly inspired by Westerns – the Lucky Seven Bar. This was owned by an immense, white-haired Lebanese who sat in a corner benignly overseeing his African staff. Country and Western music came from an African band, the members of which all wore Western outfits, down to shoestring ties and spurred heels. Monrovia after dark was beginning to feel like a poor American town.

Ephraim John, the *Observer* reporter, joined us in the Lucky Bar and later directed us to Lipps' nightclub. Noah gave up the ghost shortly after we reached there and returned to the hotel. For Ephraim, on the other hand, the night only really seemed to start in this small, crowded venue. He quickly surrendered himself to the loud soul and reggae music, like somebody seized by an irresistible impulse. He threw himself amongst the twisting, writhing bodies on the dance floor.

Meanwhile, in a remote region of Liberia, Charles Taylor, a former minister, a fugitive from American and Liberian justice, a man one Liberian described to me as being as 'crooked and vicious as Doe', was planning to march on Monrovia. In a mere matter of months, anarchy would reign and blood would flow into the Mesurado River and stain the walls of churches. The music and dancing would stop.

Maybe they knew, Ephraim and those other dancers in that nightclub. Who can say? I was certainly struck by the increasingly feverish atmosphere they generated as the place became unbearably crowded, the music louder; the dancing more vigorous. The air seemed to be filled with a ferocious determination to have a good time. I grew sleepy and weary but – completely entranced by the intensity of it all – I couldn't leave. Maybe they knew.

Despite being infected by whatever mysterious spirit enlivened the nightclub, Ephraim showed concern for my lack of participation. He disappeared for a while and returned with a girl. His arched eyebrows and conspiratorial smile, which managed to remain mischievous, signalled that she had been brought for my entertainment. A gesture typical of an African host.

Her name was Edwina and, perhaps frustrated by our attempts to talk above the music, she later suggested that we try another venue. I was agreeable. Ephraim too, as long as there would be more music and beer. So we left for the Hotel Africa. It was now about 3 a.m., but central Monrovia was still awake. Groups of people milled about outside discos and eating places. Car loads of youngsters cruised the streets. Driving past them, I wondered whether my surprise at the city's late-night liveliness was merely the reaction of a man who, galloping towards middle age, was losing his enthusiasm for chasing the night.

As we drove, Ephraim told us a story about the sea: A farmer once took the sea to court and won. The sea had risen in a storm and destroyed his crops and stolen his land. The judge threatened to dismiss the case unless the plaintiff could produce the defendant. The farmer went down to the sea, scooped up a bucketful and brought it to the court. But the judge again threatened to dismiss the case, this time on the grounds that the defendant could not speak for herself. The farmer asked the judge to accompany him down to the sea. And when the court had gathered on the beach, the farmer asked the judge to listen. Slamming his gavel down, the judge ordered silence and listened. And he heard the sea lashing against distant rocks and pounding the shoreline. The sea spoke. It was found guilty and ordered to compensate the farmer.

It was much easier to talk in the disco of the Hotel Africa. It was several miles from central Monrovia and far less crowded. Ephraim again quickly leapt on to the dance floor, leaving me alone with Edwina.

Edwina turned out to be an extremely serious young lady. She was in her early twenties and had a two-year-old son whose father had long disappeared to Abidjan, where, she believed, he now drove a taxi. Pregnancy had irreparably disrupted her life, prematurely ending her schooling and for a while estranging her from her family. Her aunt, with whom she lived, had thrown her out and for some months during her pregnancy she lived in Freetown, Sierra Leone, with her boyfriend. When the relationship collapsed, she returned to

Monrovia and relatives persuaded the aunt to take her back.

She regarded motherhood as a curse. Without exam certificates, she was unlikely to find decent work. She was an intelligent girl, with a patina of polish which seemed to heighten the familiar tragedy that was her life: a future forestalled in a moment of sexual recklessness. Now she peddled the very pleasure that had caused her downfall. She did this discreetly, relying on friends for introductions to foreigners.

She did not volunteer her story. I prompted its telling. But I wasn't prepared for the effect it had on me. It stirred a dangerous mixture of sympathy and desire; I wanted both to help and possess her. As this confused swirl of emotions passed, I recognised the hopelessness of her position, and felt vaguely ashamed at my other, less than noble, though natural, impulse. I suddenly asked her to dance. Somehow it seemed safer on the dance floor.

We left Hotel Africa just before dawn. After some coffee at an all-night café, we dropped Edwina home. Before leaving the car, she gave me a photograph of herself, dressed in Kente cloth. I offered her some money 'for her son'. But she refused it, saying, 'I want you to remember me as a friend in Monrovia.' Then she lightly kissed my cheek and was gone.

Ephraim, who'd been drinking steadily for hours, was remarkably sober. We talked for a while before parting and he said he was sure that I would one day return to Liberia. I said I hoped so, and we shook hands firmly and my eyes moistened. I watched him climb into a cab and realised that within a week he had, wittingly or unwittingly, placed me in two highly emotional situations. If he hadn't gone charging into the Minister of Information's house, Noah and I may not have quarrelled, at least not so quickly and so intensely. The other was his introduction to Edwina. Ephraim and Monrovia seemed synonymous.

When I got back to my hotel room, I was far too tired to sleep. I'd packed, but for a few items, and the car taking us to Freetown would soon arrive. From the balcony of my room, wearied by a night for Nelson Mandela, I savoured the startling freshness of this African morning, and noticed the choppy waves on the Atlantic Ocean. Then a mysterious sadness washed over me and the morning suddenly tasted bittersweet.

THREE

MONROVIA TO FREETOWN

I'd not slept all night and was feeling agreeably bluesy as the taxi sped towards the city limits of Monrovia. The city was still asleep but here and there women laden with produce made their way to market. Beyond the settlement villages, the land flattened and impenetrable bushes of dazzling verdancy grew on both sides of the road, blocking all view of the landscape. Occasionally we passed through rubber farms and the silver-grey trunks of their tall, slender trees glistened. The road was surprisingly straight and smooth. And the Peugeot 504 station-wagon in which we were travelling devoured it greedily.

I dozed off and woke up with Noah's voice asking me for my passport. We had arrived at a police checkpoint. Men dressed in grey-blue uniforms and carrying heavy-looking, ancient rifles wandered up and down a small hill beside a police station. I shook off my drowsiness and went inside. Here an obese sergeant discreetly snatched glances of curiosity at me. His copper-coloured jowls shone in the sole lamp of a gloomy office. While he inspected our documents, I wandered to a cell behind his desk. There a young man clung to the bars and stared at and seemingly through me to the morning that was now in full flight. The pungent odour of urine floated from the cell and the prisoner. He asked me for a cigarette and I obliged him hesitantly. It crossed my mind, perhaps stained by a night of roaming a city which had at times reminded me of a B-movie, that this desperado might seize me as an hostage. But he gratefully took the cigarette and I lit it for him. I asked him how he'd landed up in this terrible place.

'I killed a man,' he said calmly.

I gulped, lost for words. He was slim and his posture, clutching the bars above his head, accentuated his stomach muscles. But he was a mere boy.

'Why now?' I asked.

'Because he was going to kill me. Woman trouble.' He shrugged his bony shoulders, as if to say 'You know how it is, man.'

The officer called my name, and I backed away from the murderer slowly. I asked the officer what would happen to the prisoner and was told that he would be taken to Monrovia, to stand trial there. Leaving the police station minutes later, I saw him still clutching the bars, his sinewy figure almost hidden by the darkness of his cell.

Nearing midday we reached the Liberia–Sierra Leone borderpost. This was sited in a shallow valley and, surrounded by the wilderness, seemed incongruous, giving a whole new meaning to a phrase I'd often heard: 'Africa's porous borders'. In the distance, on the Sierra Leone side, was a wide ochre-coloured road which climbed into dark vegetation. A stream of people flowed up and down it. The clothes of the women and children were intensely bright, almost luminous. The smell of fried fish and meat floated on the dust-filled air of the harmattan, the wind which blows off the Sahara at this time of year.

Immigration officers thoroughly searched our bags in a lengthy and exasperating exercise. While Noah dealt with the paperwork I wandered outside to sit down. There were no seats and I stood for a while gazing at the hubbub of the borderpost. An officer came on to the narrow shaded porch, a young boy carrying a chair for him. He carried a slim black stick so I figured he was a senior officer. After some minutes, he called the boy, who had taken a seat on the edge of the porch, and told him to bring me a chair. The boy brought it to where I stood. I took it gratefully as the sun was now directly over-head. But, weakened by the Monrovia night, I was too tired to be sociable. I acknowledged his kindness with a nod and we sat there on the porch beneath the midday sun.

From immigration we went to customs, which was situated directly on the bordergates. The atmosphere here was like that of a market. Women carried on their heads baskets of tomatoes and cabbages or small cages of chickens, while little girls carried bowls of fried fish and men pushed roughly made carts loaded with pineapples and potatoes. All had to pass between rows of customs officers who sat beneath thatched shades on plastic chairs. Now and again a customs officer would point his baton at a barefoot traveller and the person would stop and anxiously surrender his goods for searching. This was done perfunctorily, with the officer remaining seated, prodding the potatoes or vegetables with his baton. In one incident, an officer called a scrawny man carrying three chickens bound together at their legs. The officer looked at the chickens and said: 'Which one you go give me?' The trader painfully surveyed his chickens, and picked the leanest one. The officer shook his head and tapped the plumpest of the chickens. The trader reluctantly separated the fowl. You could almost hear the poor man's lamentation for his loss.

I witnessed several similar acts of rapacity before I had to dash to rescue my own belongings from green-eyed customs officers. My suitcase had already been searched and I hadn't expected to repeat this procedure here. But a customs officer wanted my suitcase opened. He seemed disappointed that, despite its size, it contained only clothes. Then he demanded to search my shoulder-bag. I had nothing to hide. To my annoyance he demanded that I remove my portable typewriter. He inspected it thoroughly and then – perhaps genuinely suspicious, maybe out of curiosity – asked me to show him how it worked.

It was another hour before we were allowed to leave Liberia. The customs officers seemed determined to find a reason to detain us. Watching them rummaging through my personal belongings irritated me, though they did not attempt to take anything. And I sought comfort from the memoirs of another traveller who may have passed this way centuries before:

'. . . Demba and his attendants immediately began to open

my bundles, and spread the different articles upon the floor, where they underwent a more strict examination than they had done at Joag. Everything that pleased them they took without scruple . . . Upon collecting the scattered remains of my little fortune after these people had left me, I found that as at Joag I had been plundered of half, so here, without even the shadow of accusation, I was deprived of half the remainder.' (*Travels in the Interior of Africa* by Mungo Park.)

I walked across the border and met the vehicle at the Sierra Leone gates. Here we were subjected to a similarly rigorous search and interminable form filling. Afterwards we ate a lunch of rice, dried fish and sweet potato leaves at a bar. The food revitalised me and helped placate a querulous mood which had descended during the lengthy border ordeal.

Then we were on the move again, climbing up the ochre-coloured path that had hours before seemed like a fantastic picture. The car stirred up the dust and the files of women and children, their faces and clothes stained by the earth, looked at us with otherworldly eyes.

The files thinned out until the road ahead was empty. Driving on to a stretch of tarmac, I mistakenly thought it would continue all the way to Freetown. But the tarmac soon vanished and we were on a dirt path which rose and dipped through heavily vegetated land. The road became rutted at the bottom of each dip, forcing the driver to slow down to a crawling pace. Mangrove swamps surrounded the track at these points, the roots of trees exposed above the black stagnant water like the tentacles of some terrible creature. To the sounds of unknown and unseen birds was now added the rattle and purr of our taxi. Sometimes the dense vegetation that banked the road cleared, revealing overgrown farmland or small wooden structures that seemed to serve no purpose, being too small to house a person. Shrines for gods of fertility. Clusters of simple huts or zinc-roofed houses with ornately painted verandahs, yards from the road, sited on patches of bare, red earth, flashed by intermittently. But mostly there was only the dust and the bush, its predatory branches overhanging our path, ever threatening to reclaim this feeble road.

Then we came to a river and its water was calm and green from the many plants that overhung it. The car was driven on to a simple ferry – pieces of plank bolted together – and hauled across the river, which from the centre, the sun illuminating its dark surface, seemed like a silver path wending its way through the foliage of the forest. After this crossing we did not pass any settlements for a long time. And the road seemed lonely.

We were stopped in a small town and required to show our papers. The sight of cars, trucks and mini-buses raised my hopes for a smoother ride from here on. But it was another two hours before we finally reached a tarmac surface and then, apart from a brief stretch, there was nothing to celebrate: the road collapsed at frequent intervals and the driver had to swerve round immense potholes or sudden buckled patches.

We were hoping to reach Freetown before dark but the setting sun above Bo told us this was an impossible target. When night came, the security points seemed to increase and we were stopping almost every twenty minutes. At each stop, we had to go through the same procedure: soldiers or policemen would shine lights in the car, in our faces, on our documents. Sometimes we were called by the commanding officer and asked to give a verbal reason for our passage. At one stop, the Liberian driver lost his temper and swore at a policeman. Only the most obsequious pleading, and a profuse apology, saved us from a night in the car or, worse, a cell.

We reached Freetown shortly before midnight, after sixteen hours on the road. In the hotel foyer I collapsed in the arms of a club chair, feeling as though I had just been ejected from a cement mixer.

FOUR

THE CREOLES, AND THE PRESIDENT'S PLEA

For all its countless imperfections, Monrovia had shown signs of growth, a new office block here, a new house over there. The same could not be said of Freetown. A morning of walking and driving through the centre of this other 'back to Africa' city left me with the impression of a city whose growth had occurred decades before and then ground to a halt in a fever of post-independence despair. This was not an entirely accurate impression: later I would discover the suburbs of Freetown, in the hills, on the coast, and realise that central Freetown is the victim of an extreme blight all too familiar in British cities in a milder form – inner-city decay.

My initial impression was heightened by the city's many colonial buildings. Surely no other African city has so many examples of Victorian colonial architecture? The most striking and haunting is the Freetown Court House, where errant natives and Creoles were tried by the 'civilising Britons' according to laws that bore no relation to the cultures of the indigenous peoples.

'The Law in Sierra has been corrupted by African practices,' a lawyer told me in an aside. So too has the building, which must have once been a boastful symbol of British aspirations, but which turned out to be less durable than its Victorian civilisers imagined. Now bushes grow out of its roof and the ubiquitous red dust stains its white walls. On some days, a deranged war veteran, bow-legged, stooping, stands at its entrance repeatedly saluting until sunset, like a faulty clockwork doll.

The Court House, shadowed by an immense three-hundred-year-old cotton tree – which marks the centre of Freetown – has, however, fared rather better than the nearby buildings. These two-storey wooden houses, with their crumbling verandahs laden with clothes hung out for drying, with their fading gaudy colours, look as unstable as an aged dowager reduced to impecuniosity and drunk on cheap gin. They were built as family homes by wealthy Creoles – the Sierra Leonean counterparts of the Americo-Liberians. This wholly modern tribe has its origins in the philanthropy and evangelical zeal of British anti-slavery crusaders, mainly William Wilberforce and Granville Sharp. The resultant culture was shaped by the British colonialists themselves, and the African descendants for whom Freetown was founded in 1787 on land purchased from several Temnes chiefs who ruled the coastal area. They were drawn from the Black poor of eighteenth-century London, Jamaican maroons, Nova Scotians, and a multiplicity of dislocated Africans. These Africans – principally Yorubas and Igbos – were slaves bound for the plantations of the Americas. They were recaptured by the British Navy off the West African coast and given freedom in Freetown. Here their speech, dress, and religion became indistinguishable from those of the settlers.

The Creole-built houses are now tenements, and some descendants of the original occupants have fled the humid heat of the coast for the cool of the hills. There, parishes with names like York, Leicester and Wellington, have the calm gentility of towns in rural England. An atmosphere accentuated by the omnipresent grey light caused by the harmattan, which shortens the day, like winter. Narrow lanes, though mercilessly pot-holed, wind through lush green land of citrus trees and guava bushes. High gates and hedges partly conceal pastoral cottages or simple but large residences at the end of long driveways. Up in the hills, the stench and poverty, the ruins and corruption of Freetown seem to belong to another country.

In contrast to the Americo-Liberians, the Creoles did not create an independent nation. They were sandwiched between the British colonial rulers and the natives. They resented the prejudices of the former which restricted them to low-level administrative positions in the colonial bureaucracy. While their British-style education – accompanied by a flamboyant mimicry of English sartorial taste – gave them a sense of superiority over the natives, or 'up-country folk'.

Under colonial rule the Creoles were relentless and articulate champions of independence. They published newspapers and pamphlets, organised trade unions, fomented unrest and were generally a thorn in the side of the colonial powers. As independence approached, they considered themselves natural heirs to the departing British colonial rulers. But they were far outnumbered by the natives – mostly Mendes and Temnes, the largest tribes in Sierra Leone – who have ruled since 1961.

One effect of native, as opposed to Creole, rule is that relations between the two groups are less marked by the tension and bitterness which contributed to the fall of the Americo-Liberians in Liberia. None the less, some Creoles do believe that the 'natives' have made a complete mess of independence.

Emile Carr, a retired Civil Servant, is a very large, very dark man who, to my eyes, looked like any other African. I spoke to him in his home in Freetown. We sat in the hall-size living-room, lit by candles because the electricity had failed, as it did around this hour every evening. Outside, children played ring-a-ring-a roses.

I had been in Freetown for three days and almost every conversation I had had touched on the debilitating and pervasive effects of corruption in the city. I asked Mr Carr whether Sierra Leone, compared to other African countries, is uniquely corrupt.

'I don't think it is more extreme here than elsewhere in Africa,' he replied. 'Before independence, this was not a corrupt society. I always think that there is one thing wrong with independence in Sierra Leone: the right people did not succeed the White man.

'Before independence there was this qualification for voting, educational qualification, property qualification. But when the White man was going, they left us with one man, one vote; and so the people who were not trained for independence over-

whelmed us. That is what has brought all this corruption and all
this bad practice.'

'Who was trained for independence?' I asked.

'The slaves who were returned from slavery and were educated people. They were educated and they were in the Civil
Service; they knew about government. With independence we
got one man, one vote; then the illiterate man took over.'

Astonished by what sounded to me like bigotry, I asked Mr
Carr whether he wasn't simply voicing Creole prejudices of the
natives.

He said: 'I don't think it is. Because when the Creoles were
educated they encouraged the people from the hinterland. Some
were brought to serve as wards and they were put to school.
And, in fact, some of them are claiming to be Creoles; they
have adopted Creole names.'

This response implied that the natives were not yet ready to
rule. But surely the Creoles remained the dominant force in the
Civil Service long after independence?

'Yes, but the nepotism came on quickly because the people
who were in the leadership wanted to bring in their people. And
so people who were not trained for the Civil Service were put
into positions of trust. You see, the politicians played on the
fears of the people. They convinced their people that the
Creoles would not serve them. They tried to convince them
that they would serve them better. They promised them all
sorts of things. So when these politicians came to power, these
people who they had made all those promises to, they invaded
their offices, asking for money for family, money to educate
their children.'

I suggested that maybe the alien character of the Civil Service
and this implanted modern state contributed to the appalling
level of corruption that now blighted the country.

He partly agreed and said: 'They used to say in general
terms, you [the Creoles] enjoyed before under the colonial
days, it's I who want to enjoy now.'

There was in this last statement a note of resignation, as
though independence under native rule couldn't have been any
different. It was all part of the order of things, immutable; men

merely obeying a natural instinct to pursue their own selfish interest. A fundamental truth illustrated by the anthropomorphic tales of Africa.

Emile Carr was a storehouse of such tales and related a few to me: One day Leopard, Wolf and Goat went hunting. Leopard's speed and ferocity enabled them to get a lot of spoils. When they returned home, Leopard left the other two, saying, 'I'm going to have a bath.' When he came back he saw that they had shared the spoils into four parts. He said: 'Oh, you have shared it into four parts, but it's three of us.' They said: 'Yes, because you are our leader we reserve two for you and the other two for ourselves.' Leopard said: 'Good. You are very sensible. Now who has got this one?' He pointed to Wolf's share. 'Oh, it's me, sah,' Wolf said. To which Leopard replied: 'All right, put it here. I provided the ammunition and that's my share for providing the ammunition.' Then he pointed to Goat's share and said, 'I led you to the hunting, so I am entitled to that and the skin of the beast and I dare you to say anything. Now get out.' And Goat and Wolf slunk off with their tails between their legs.

A less cruel, modern variation on the same story goes: The president and the politician, the economist and the permanent secretary were considering awarding a contract. Aware of the possible kickback from the contract, the president wanted to choose the members of his delegation with care. So he asked the economist: 'two and two'. The economist replied: 'Four, sir.' 'OK fine, wait outside,' the president said. He then asked the permanent secretary 'Two and two', who said, 'Anyone you say, sir.' 'Fine, wait outside,' the president said. He then asked the politician 'Two and two'. 'Three for you and one for me, sir,' the politician said. 'You'll get the job,' said the president.

From what I'd seen and heard in Liberia, I had no reason to believe that Mr Carr's Creole-ruled Sierra Leone would have been a vast improvement. His suggestion that under the Creoles Sierra Leone would be less corrupt was laughable. I considered Sierra Leone fortunate, despite its widespread corruption, which probably appeared worse than elsewhere because of the country's size. It had avoided the groundswell of tribal resentment which contributed to the fall of the Americo-Liberians and the birth of Samuel Doe's government, plunging Liberia into a decade of coups and now a possible fratricidal civil war. I had come to the conclusion – and not without a measure of disappointment – that in both countries the descendants of returned Africans are minorities separated from other Africans by history and culture. They are tribes, as distinct as all the other African tribes. And in a political environment where ethnic allegiances are so important, tribal minorities which insist on ruling inevitably court disaster. Mercifully, Creoles who continue to believe in their natural right to rule are probably in a minority.

Why, though, did the Creoles and their Americo-Liberian counterparts not simply melt into the local African population? In both countries, long after arriving, the returned Africans seem to have clung tenaciously to the hybrid culture they brought from the West. It is only in the latter part of this century that they have begun to take pride in the African aspects of their culture.

A century after the founding of Sierra Leone in 1787, numerous English travellers couldn't resist critically commenting on the Creoles' fondness for mimicking the British. The Victorian traveller Sir Richard Burton, for example, wrote of 'savvy niggers' on the coast, who were 'inferior to the uncontaminated natives of the hinterland'. Travelling Britons were not the only critics of the Creoles. The settlers themselves generated a robust literature of self-criticism. One Creole critic dismissed his own people as those 'hybridised, transmogrified, and passionate borrowers of Western values, ideas, norms, mores, thought patterns, religion and cosmology', who appeared to have 'been doped by the White man's religion and civilisation'.

*   *   *

One of the Creoles' harshest critics was Edward Wilmot Blyden, a nineteenth-century nationalist who believed that the Creoles' future lay in forging stronger links with Africans from the interior and adopting Islam. His great-grandson, Edward Wilmot Blyden III, lives close to central Freetown on sloping land which enjoys the breeze from the hills. I visited Mr Blyden to find out about his great-grandfather and also to get his views on why Creole assimilation had been so slow.

It was late afternoon when we called on Mr Blyden. He was still having his siesta. While a young boy, with slim, sleek legs in khaki pants, went to wake him, we waited under a sprawling mango tree, its leaves laden with the dust of the harmattan, shadowing the house with ageing majesty. The road was steep and I imagined that many a midday walker stopped here for a rest under the shade. Nearby two women sat behind a rough wooden table, selling cigarettes and sweets. A child played on the ground at their feet. And because it was nearly evening, the sun was seemingly equidistant between the sea and the sky; and that unique smell of the African evening – the dust, a faint trace of roasting meat and fish – clung to the air.

While waiting there, under the mango tree, I saw a stooped old man with spindly bow-legs and mistakenly thought it was Mr Blyden. He turned out to be a Mr Jarret, and he lived in a small zinc-roofed house beside Mr Blyden's more impressive home. He told me he was born in 1916 and his parents came from Barbados. Mr Jarret was proud of his West Indian origins but was more concerned with surviving the economic horrors of Freetown. How did he survive from day to day?

'That's the problem,' he said, laughing, and his wrinkled, leathery face came alive. 'That's the hardest question to answer. We live by providence. We live by divine providence. My wife died two years ago. I only live by whisky. I only sell one beer and one stout.'

I now realised that the first room of the little house was a shop. Glancing inside I saw shelves empty, but for the odd bottle of beer.

'We are living in a hard time,' he said. 'A very hard time.'

'You were born in 1916 under colonial rule. Do you ever find yourself regretting the departure of the British?' I asked.

'Oh, I was very happy in the colonial days. What they did was very good for me. But in Africa in general they wanted independence. They're just like a child. When he's born he says "I aim to take my own way". Just like the prodigal son. He says he wants to be by himself. So the father says all right you can go, or he says don't go. Wait until you're ripe. The son will say "no I am ripe". When he has gone and everything is gone he says I will arise and go to my father.'

I didn't get a chance to ask Mr Jarret if he believed Sierra Leone should return to the father. He was an old man; the best days of his life had been spent in the colonial days. It seemed to me that he would remember them as a golden age.

Mr Blyden came shortly. His house was a modern version of the crumbling Victorian-built Creole house – a verandah ran its length. We spoke in his study, a cool, small room, and Mr Blyden sat in an antique Queen Anne chair brought back, he revealed, from Russia, where he had served as Ambassador for his country.

He was a small dapper man with a professorial air, lively eyes and a wry smile. He spoke enthusiastically about his great-grandfather. 'He would weep if he saw the state of modern Africa, the instability, the lack of development,' Mr Blyden said despairingly.

Mr Blyden's great-grandfather was born in the then Danish-controlled island of St Thomas – part of the Virgin Islands – and migrated to Liberia in 1862. There he enjoyed a varied working life as a journalist, Presbyterian clergyman, educationalist and statesman.

Edward Wilmot Blyden's writings made him the leading African intellectual of the nineteenth century. He wrote extensively about the 'Negro Personality' in an effort to refute the many European myths about African civilisation, or the lack of it. He is undoubtedly the forerunner to twentieth-century figures like Marcus Garvey, and his ideas anticipate those of the Negritude writers in Francophone Africa.

Mr Blyden explained that his great-grandfather's criticism of the Creoles was based on his objection to the strong European influence in their culture, which distinguished them from native Africans: 'This acculturation bothered him. He believed that the Black man had lost his soul, lost his identity, lost his personality through this acculturation.' The Creoles, Edward Wilmot Blyden argued, could only regain their African personality by abandoning Christianity, which demanded servitude of Africans, and embracing Islam, which encouraged Africans to assert themselves. Mr Blyden implied that his great-grandfather's argument was less pertinent today because there was a high level of intermarriage between Creoles and natives.

Some days after speaking to Edward Wilmot Blyden III, I wondered why his great-grandfather appeared to ignore the indigenous expressions of African culture. After all, Islam is just another foreign religion. It was Mr McCaulay who prompted this belated thought. More importantly, he also, indirectly, provided an answer to the puzzle of why Creole culture had survived such a long time.

Mr McCaulay was an optician. On the morning after my rocky journey to Freetown, rattled but rested, I was looking over the balcony to the sea when a lens from my glasses fell out and smashed on some red rocks below. Mr McCaulay, who worked in a public eye clinic in Kissi, made me a new lens. He had trained in London, and wore dazzling silver-framed spectacles, which could only have been kept in such pristine condition by assiduous polishing.

As a gesture of appreciation for the speed with which he had completed the work, I treated Mr McCaulay to a meal at Solar Restaurant on Cape Sierra. It was night and a strong breeze blew off the sea. We had eaten a meal prepared by the African-American chef and owner, Kofi, a tall, straight, brown-skinned man of regal dignity. The meal – I ate steamed Atlantic sole garnished with herbs and spices – had been served by Kofi's wives, two stunningly beautiful women from Chicago. Both wives, Mr McCaulay told me enviously, were business graduates.

Mr McCaulay spoke expansively about the difficult times Sierra Leone was going through. He had his eyes on another professional course in Britain, perhaps accountancy: 'I don't know a poor accountant,' he said.

He was keen to find out about accountancy courses in
London. But I couldn't help him with any tips. Besides, I wanted
to talk about Sierra Leone. I'd earlier seen in Sierra Leone's
National Museum the frightening costume of the bundu priest-
ess – all black, body-length straw and a large black mask. As
this recent visit was fresh in my mind, I asked Mr McCaulay to
tell me about secret societies.

The question seemed to enliven him, ending the dirge of
hardship that he had been singing most of the evening. He
spoke with great intensity, describing membership of the Poro
(the society for men) as a mandatory sign of manhood. The
initiation rites involved two years of seclusion in the bush,
where boys were taught the songs of adulthood, the arts of
war and the laws governing everyday life. Mr McCaulay said
emphatically: 'If you don't belong to a secret society, you don't
belong. You're nobody.' If a member transgressed the society's
rules, he was punished severely, regardless of status. It was
not unknown for 'chiefs to be tied up and left in the sun for
days'. Revealing the secrets of the society could result in death
and most certainly ostracism. Punishment disgraced the entire
family and members were known to die from grief.

Mr McCaulay would say no more than that. The evening
ended on a note of grave silence. I sensed that perhaps he felt
he had said too much. Yet this initially quite casual conversation
was one of the most revealing I'd had so far. It had never
occurred to me that amongst native Africans there were certain
important arcane cultural practices which might exclude repatri-
ated Africans. Mr McCaulay's silence made me feel like a
stranger. And it seemed to me then that there existed an
ancient, deep and obscure part of Africa for ever closed to me.
Perhaps the African descendants who returned centuries before
felt the same way.

*   *   *

In Liberia my enquiries into the fate of Americo-Liberians had been overshadowed by a looming political crisis. Similarly, in Sierra Leone, as I (with my producer) went about the daily task of conducting interviews about the Creoles, the country's urgent problems impressed themselves on me. There was no escaping the signs of a nation locked in a vicious cycle of poverty, debt and political ineptitude.

The depth of Sierra Leone's economic crisis was evident in several facets of everyday life. Mile-long queues of cars often extended from petrol stations. Drivers left their cars overnight if unsuccessful in buying petrol. It was not uncommon for the car to remain in a queue for a week. One day the arrival of a petrol tanker in Freetown Harbour caused tremendous excitement throughout the city. This mood even survived the revelation that the tanker's captain refused to discharge his cargo until he had been paid. All imports were paid cash on delivery. The nation was bankrupt.

Sierra Leone has long been a great exporter of people. It was from the Sierra Leone coastline that John Hawkins, in 1562, sailed with the first shipload of slaves for the New World. And the Creoles are famous for their migratory habits. For many, Sierra Leone was just a point of re-entry to Africa, and they soon settled elsewhere on the continent, in places like Nigeria, Ghana and The Gambia. Others became sailors, forming the basis of early British Black communities in seaports like Liverpool and Cardiff. But in recent years middle-class flight from the everyday horrors of an impoverished country has resulted in a brain drain. Britain and, increasingly, the United States are the favourite destinations of the educated.

Those forced to remain, the poor, the uneducated, put their faith in God or Allah. Theirs is a powerful faith. It helps them survive overnight food price rises, erratic electricity supply, a constant shortage of kerosene for cooking, and the daily rumours of politicians or Civil Servants who abscond with huge sums of public money. It also gave people a placid patience, which I found almost as harrowing as the privations they had to endure.

Many Sierra Leoneans blamed the country's misfortunes on the Lebanese. 'The Arabs' were held responsible for creating

a powerful black market by hoarding basic commodities. They
were even held responsible for personal misfortunes. One afternoon, while waiting for Noah near the British High Commission,
I was approached by a beggar. He was a wretched-looking man
with ragged clothes, a shuffling walk and pathetic eyes. He
showered me with blessings from God and Allah. Then he told
me that he had once been a driver for a wealthy Lebanese
businessman. His descent into the gutter of life began after he
killed a Lebanese boy in a road accident. Since that day, the
boy's family and his former employer had persecuted him,
ensuring that he could not work.

The Lebanese are, indeed, a powerful group here. They
control the country's distribution network and undoubtedly help
to create artificial scarcities which result in inflation. But to
solely blame them for the shambolic state of the Sierra Leonean
economy seemed, to me, little more than scapegoating.

The country's small liberal intelligentsia, however, pointed
accusative fingers at the current President, Joseph Momoh, and
the one-party political system bequeathed by his predecessor
Siaka 'Pa' Stevens.

'Pa' Stevens retired from office in 1985 and has since become
the subject of a powerful mythology. A hardback comic book
sold cheaply all over Freetown, titled *Once upon a time . . .
Sierra Leone and a President called Siaka Stevens*, recounts the
slave trade, colonialism, and then Stevens' birth in terms which
portray him as a modern-day redeemer, the father of the nation.

Independence and democracy (in 1961) got off to a shaky
start in Sierra Leone. Widespread ballot rigging, bribery and
violence by the Sierra Leone People's Party made elections a
farce. In 1967 Stevens' All People's Congress managed to beat
the SLPP at the polls. Rather than relinquish power, the
defeated Premier, Sir Albert Margai, instigated a military coup
and the army imposed martial law.

Stevens fled into exile and returned a year later, following
another coup. Reinstated as Prime Minister, he swiftly moved
to centralise power and suppress all opposition parties, largely
through intimidation and violence. Multi-partyism was abandoned in 1978 on the grounds that the young nation was not

yet ready for such a sophisticated political system because it generated tribalism and violence.

Years after his retirement and death, Stevens' critics are more than ever convinced that the one-party system was a grave mistake, reducing the country to abject poverty.

Patrick Foray, Principal of Fourah Bay College and a former Foreign Minister, told me: 'I refused to accept the suggestion that the people who put the APC into power in sixty-seven, sixty-eight, sixty-nine were too illiterate to understand the implications of voting on party lines. I refuse also to accept the suggestion that the multi-party system fosters ethnicity. These are merely excuses people are giving for the one-party system. The wounds in the country really began with the tampering with the political system.'

By denying the people a choice of parties the new system has allowed power to be concentrated in the hands of a few powerful individuals who are not subject to public accountability. One-party rule, contrary to its stated intentions, has also exacerbated ethnic tension. President Momoh is reportedly surrounded by ethnic war-lords in the form of the Ekutay – an ethnic cabal dominated by members of the Limba tribe – which makes all the major decisions of state.

Access to political office, which almost guarantees wealth, is now sought with an amoral desperation. *The Shaft* – one of the country's leading newspapers, which none the less looks worse than a poorly produced student rag – one day carried this horrific report:

'Police investigating one of the most sordid cases of cannibalism in Moyamba district have arrested and detained nine suspects who are alleged to have eaten part of the body of a thirteen-year-old girl. While villages were celebrating Christmas the girl was sold to Sorie Conteh by her aunt for 6,000 leones. Conteh allegedly wanted to perform a human sacrifice to ensure his success in the township elections.'

The traditional had corrupted the modern and vice versa.

President Joseph Saidu Momoh also owes his position to the corrupting clash between old and new. For the one-party state blends the traditional authority of the chief with the modern

authority of an elected office. So President Momoh looks like a
chief, albeit a benign one.

I met him in the presidential office, situated in an ancient
castle, a former slave fort. He wore a burgundy-coloured jacket,
which seemed a size too small, and his smooth, bulbous cheeks
glowed healthily. He played with his fat hands as we spoke. It
was difficult to imagine that this dandified, gauche man had
once been a soldier, Sandhurst-trained. Rather he reminded me
powerfully of some of Nigeria's pleasure-loving Emirs.

The President, not without sincerity, was quick to reaffirm
his total agreement with the 'views expressed by my predecessor, the late Doctor Siaka Stevens: in our part of the world,
if we attempt to go back into a multi-party form of government,
there is no way we can do it without having the parties established on tribal lines, regional lines, ethnic lines. It is just not
possible. By doing that we will further be dividing the country.'

The basic act of enfranchisement, he implied, was far too
complex for his average compatriot. It required literacy and in
a country where 'sixty to seventy per cent of the people are
illiterate, the whole system collapses from the start. For our
stage of development I think the one-party system is more
appropriate.'

Nevertheless, President Momoh insisted that his country's
one-party system was 'first and foremost most democratic. For
example, we allow freedom of speech. As of today we are
operating no less than nineteen newspapers, and most of the
newspapers carry articles fairly very much critical even about
the government and at times even about me as President.

'We have a very, very democratic parliamentary system
where members of the back-benches speak freely and take
ministers to task. Quite a good number of ministers have lost
their portfolios as a result of the heavy attacks made on them
by back-benchers. We have a judiciary that is very, very much
independent; we conduct elections regularly. And even in the
present one-party system we allow as many as five candidates
to contest in one constituency when we have general elections.
So in that case I don't think that there is anything that could be
more democratic.'

'But', I interjected, 'how could five members from the same party possibly give the electorate real choices.'

'It doesn't worry me that because five candidates come from the same party therefore all five must have the same views on the same issues. They will be five different people with different backgrounds: academic achievements, government training. You may have a candidate who is a graduate from the Soviet Union, a graduate from Britain, from the United States; somebody who has not been abroad at all. So they all meet, and it is interesting to go to Parliament and hear all the discourse. Their views usually differ very, very widely.'

The President felt it necessary to remind me that before 1961 'there was nothing like any political system of government here. The only government that was known was Her Majesty's Government, who had British administrators – District Officers, Provincial Secretaries and Judges.'

He argued that colonialism was the beginning of one-party democracy. 'It was when the White man was taking his exit, when we were beginning to think about independence that we did what you called the Westminster type of politics. It was introduced lock, stock and barrel!

'So overnight we found ourselves being called upon to practise a system which was totally novel to us. And speaking very, very frankly, since then we have not been able to get over that difficulty.

'This may well be one of the reasons why politics in the developing countries is so violent. We have been called upon to practise a system of government of which we are totally ignorant and which is altogether alien to us.'

The President then assumed a tone of mocking nostalgia for the days of colonial rule. The simplicity of it. 'We were very comfortable under the colonial administrator. He was the absolute authority. The District Commissioner sent people to jail, freed people, banished people. His authority was absolute. They were able to rule for over one hundred and fifty years with that system in this country. So there are times when we wish that they had left that system with us.'

The new system, President Momoh said, not only generated

tribal conflict, it also pitted the authority of parliamentarians against that of chiefs. 'In most of our areas up country, the provinces, there is this conflict of authority between the Member of Parliament and the paramount chief. You still have the old colonial type of paramount chief who feels he's the absolute authority. Then you have the Member of Parliament who says I'm the parliamentary appointed representative of my people, so I am the boss. It is one of our sharpest conflicts in the provinces. And this is just one of the creations of our colonial masters. Fortunately for them this was not in existence while they administered.'

Since entering Sierra Leone, I had begun to encounter the French, and mindful that after this stop I would be entering the Francophone zone, I introduced this theme into our interview. France has a far closer relationship to its former West African colonies than Britain. So I asked President Momoh whether the Anglophone countries have benefited from being left to stand on their own two feet by their former colonial masters.

His reply was serious and emphatic: '. . . definitely not. There are people like us who because of a very close affinity to the British feel very, very sad that after independence Britain just decided to sort of abandon us, so to speak. With these new systems after independence we needed the experience of the old colonial master to guide us until we actually got into full maturity. But to have abandoned us at that stage and then on to this point, I think it's most unfortunate.

'You see, we need godfathers. Sadly, we of the Anglophone world don't seem to have such godfathers. And this is why we envy our French counterparts. They enjoy quite a lot of backing and assistance from the French which unfortunately we don't get at all.'

Surprised by this confession of weakness (with its disturbing echo of my brief conversation with the ageing Mr Jarret) I asked the President whether his nation did not enjoy greater national pride as a result of its greater self-reliance, even if it was proving to be difficult.

'I don't think there's anybody who enjoys hurting himself all the time,' President Momoh said after a moment's thought.

'Because when you get up you stumble, you hit your head, and then you bruise yourself. I don't think there's anything pleasant or enjoyable about that. Right now we are lying flat on the ground and we have a problem getting up. God knows we have the intention, the desire to actually get up. But against that we have heavy forces that are pressing us down. So even with all the efforts we are making to get up on our own, there are heavy forces that are pressing us down. I'm talking economically: the unfair commodities prices, the huge debts; you can go on and on. So what we need is somebody who will just reach out and give us a lift. Lift us a bit and allow us to stand on our feet.'

Up until this moment I'd regarded President Momoh as a complacent, benevolent dictator. But his answer moved me.

His was the voice of an Africa still encumbered by the Black man's burden: the selfishness and greed of a Western world, the White world, indifferent to the suffering caused by its ruthless pursuit of profit. The foundations of so much Western wealth had been built on his people's back through the slave trade, then colonialism, now the debt trap. His entreaty offended something in me – my racial pride? – yet I could not deny that he had sound historical and moral rights to plead for his beleaguered people, and to be heard by the West.

FIVE

LOOKING FOR GRAHAM GREENE

Albert Fereira managed the City Hotel, and as business was slow, he could comfortably pass the day on his back. Sometimes he was forced to brush away a pestering fly with his bony hand of loose, mottled and dry skin. He would do so in gestures of almost languorous indifference. Now and then he had to mildly scold the gang of golden-skinned children – some his grand-children – who noisily played around him. On the whole though life made no excessive demands on the manager. I once caught the normally laconic Mr Fereira in a good mood and he remin-isced on an age when sailors and spies and Graham Greene drank at his bar.

Graham Greene's *The Heart of the Matter* opens with Wilson, a spy, waiting for 'gin and bitters' on the balcony of what the novel calls the Bedford Hotel.

It was difficult to imagine an agent of Her Majesty's Intelli-gence Service staying there now. The courtyard was bare and dusty; the balcony's only seating a wobbly, cushionless stool, thrown out from the empty bar below, where the septuagen-arian Swiss-born manager passed the hot, stagnant afternoons under a creaky rusting fan which whirred with sluggish futility.

Mr Fereira did not remember much about Graham Greene himself and he considered *The Heart of the Matter* 'too one-sided'. He was reluctant or unable to elaborate on what pre-cisely he disliked about Greene's famous novel. Perhaps a younger Mr Fereira held passionate, detailed views about that work of fiction, but this older, supine Mr Fereira had energy only for vague reminiscences of characters and atmosphere.

Yet his terse criticism of *The Heart of the Matter* had some truth. Greene's gloomy novel, set during the Second World War, belongs in the Conradian tradition of European fiction with an African scenery. Its Africans are invisible, shadowy figures in a background against which an archetypal Greene story about love, faith and moral decay unfolds. The Africans are highlighted only as dishonest, cruel or showing dog-like loyalty to a European master. When the brooding protagonist – Scobie, a colonial policeman – commits suicide, the reader is left feeling that this ultimate sin was due as much to his moral weakness as a corrupt and powerfully corrupting climate.

Still, I must admit that I enjoyed Greene's novel: it was like a good stiff drink, a vintage whisky, the taste of which lingered on the tongue long after finishing it. If Greene failed to rise entirely above the prejudices of his age, his novel's impressions of colonial Sierra Leone's moral climate has a modern resonance. Blessed, or cursed, with abundant deposits of gold and diamonds, this minuscule West African state continues to attract professional diamond smugglers who are assisted by eager local politicians and Civil Servants.

So I regarded the City Hotel as a literary landmark. I went there as often as possible, with vague hopes of meeting smugglers, perhaps even the odd Briton who had resisted the impulse to flee when independence came.

Geoffrey Cargill was the closest I came to a Briton. He grew up in east London and belonged to the 'lowest ranks' (his own description) of urban workers in Freetown. He sold loose cigarettes, kola-nuts, oranges, chewing gum and sweets from a makeshift stall outside the hotel, and lived in its basement. He was of small stature and yet his head and hands were incongruously large, like someone who had suffered from frequent life-threatening illnesses, almost like one of those child famine victims seen in pictures appealing for aid for Africa. But he was perky, lively and laughed easily. Shortly after meeting him he told me this Freetown anecdote:

When God created Sierra Leone, he poured into the land

diamonds and gold and constant sunshine and into the ocean an inexhaustible supply of fish. The Angel Gabriel, surprised by the Almighty's magnanimity, asked why the Lord had been so generous: wasn't it unfair to the less well-endowed nations? The Almighty answered: 'Wait. You haven't seen the people I'm going to put there.'

I was immediately drawn to Geoffrey Cargill. Although we were about the same age, I recognised in him my younger restless self, fragmented, alienated from Britain, searching in Africa for something that I could not name. But my own quest had neither been so extended nor taken such an oblique, circuituous route as his.

Geoffrey Cargill was born in Jamaica and brought to London as an eight-year-old. After dropping out of the sixth-form, he wandered around London for years, then joined the Hare Krishna movement which sent him first to India, then Kenya and Nigeria. Horrified by Lagos, he fled – 'for my sanity' – and landed in Freetown. He had been there four years.

He was growing disillusioned with the Hare Krishna movement. His waning faith was not unconnected with a burning desire to return to Britain. But a major obstacle stood in his path: he had never taken out British citizenship and therefore had no automatic right of re-entry. For the past two years he and his mother had been corresponding regularly about this problem. She still lived in the East End and sometimes enclosed a ten-pound note in her letter. He walked with her latest letter for weeks, and showed me one. Geoffrey longed to see her, his sister, his brother, and his first nephew 'Shaka'. Ironically, he was curious as to why his nephew had been given an African name. Had he himself not come to Africa in search of his own name?

Geoffrey's wife, a petite, ebony-dark woman of preternatural beauty, was also a follower of Hare Krishna. In fact, she kept alive his little remaining faith: 'She thinks I am stupid wanting to go back to London,' he told me. 'Sometimes she keeps my letters from my mother. Sometimes I feel that she's keeping me a prisoner here.'

One night Geoffrey told me in a conspiratorial voice: 'When

I was younger, in London, it used to bother me that Africans had sold us into slavery. Really trouble me. How could they do such a thing. But I understand now. How it could happen. The slave trade is still alive here,' he said. 'The Africans sell their children to the Lebanese. The children grow up as slaves. There is so much poverty and ugliness here.'

'Is there no beauty at all?' I replied.

'There is. It's like the beauty of the lotus blossom, the supreme flower, a flower that grows only in mud.'

Geoffrey and his wife took it in turns, at four-hour intervals, to run their stall. They kept it open throughout the night. I sat with Geoffrey on two nights. Long periods would pass without a customer; and when someone did emerge from the syrupy darkness the value of their purchases hardly seemed to make this nocturnal vigil worthwhile. A single cigarette, matches, a stick of chewing gum. Occasionally, a customer would linger and make small talk in the Creole patois which Geoffrey spoke fluently. That was how I met Geoffrey's friend, Billy. I was introduced by Geoffrey as his 'Jamaican brother'.

Billy was about thirteen or fourteen and had come to buy a cigarette. Although the night air was chilly, because of the harmattan, he wore only a thin T-shirt, khaki short pants and rubber slippers. His eyes were narrow, dark slits, his head shaven. He smelled strongly of sweat. Billy lived on the streets.

His English was difficult to understand but I gathered that he had been on the streets for two years. He was born in Nagon and had lived all over the country with different relatives before coming to Freetown. Here, he survived by 'dregging' or hustling. This ranged from running errands for market women, shopkeepers and fishermen to stealing. He picked pockets, pilfered from the market women. He had sold '*diamba*' (cannabis) and worked as a pimp, providing girls for tourists or sailors. 'We row them in canoes to the ship. Girls not always want pay. So maybe we stop in the water. Ask for money there. If they don't want pay, we rock the canoe. Then they pay.' He laughed a mature, cruel, male laugh.

'Don't you ever sleep?' I asked him.

He shrugged his slender shoulders. 'When I chop, well, well,' he said and laughed again, rubbing his stomach.

'So you haven't chopped tonight?'

'Yes. But food no good. Done give me bellyache.'

Geoffrey offered to sell him an Anadin tablet.

He declined and began talking about food. Billy got his meals from a variety of sources. Rubbish bins in desperate times. His favourite source was the '*Pul na do*', a celebration. When he and his friends heard of a '*Pul na do*' ceremony, they attended. 'We just wait until they bring the rice, then we would eat. We used to eat so much rice at these "*Pul na do*".'

I asked him how he had learnt to survive on the streets. He told me that when he first came to Freetown after running away from home, he almost starved. 'I could not dreg. I suffered from hungry. I was getting craw-craw. Then I met a Bra, Mohammed. He teach me everything. How to steal at Kenema Market. The places to sleep. You know, the filling stations, the bus station.'

But his Bra had become greedy and wanted almost all the money he, Billy, made. 'Mohammed had many, many boys working for him. He had a room at Sawpit. Every night we must give him something. We have nothing, he chase us away; maybe he beat us before.

'One day I steal a goat and took it to Mohammed. He gave me plenty leones. But the police came for the goat. They took Mohammed away with the goat. When he came back, he beat me. He beat me very, very much. Ever since I leave him. I find another Bra to protect me. Abibu. He chased Mohammed when he come to make trouble for me.'

Billy asked me about Jamaica and London. I told him that Kingston was like Freetown, with its heat and mountains. London, I told him, was very different, big with a wide river and glass buildings that almost touched the clouds. I said that in London a boy his age could not live on the streets; the law would not allow it. He would be placed in a government home and schooled.

He said there were such homes in Freetown. But he had heard terrible things about them and preferred the streets. His only regret was that he had stopped school – which he used to enjoy – because he knew that to 'get book' would be good. Nevertheless, he hoped one day to meet a girl and 'fall in love and marry her and have plenty children. Maybe I'll drive a Pujero.' (The Pujero is a Japanese jeep, ideal for the Sierra Leonean roads, beloved by the wealthy here.) He mimed holding a steering-wheel and assumed a haughty posture. 'On Sundays we drive to Lumley Beach and eat rice and chicken and swim.' He laughed again and his laughter saddened me.

Presently, a trio of ragged boys came to buy cigarettes. They were Billy's friends and he said he would leave with them for Government Wharf, where a night-watchman had promised them somewhere to sleep.

As he walked away I asked him if his stomach felt better. He grinned stoically, shook his head and said: 'It's not easy to be a man in this Freetown-O.' And with his motley crew, he disappeared into the night, a child for whom there had been no childhood.

Not all Geoffrey's friends were so vulnerable or voluble. A tall, thin African-American who lived in the City Hotel and described himself as a musician eyed me suspiciously. Within minutes of our meeting, he made a feeble excuse and vanished. I never saw him again, despite my numerous visits to the hotel.

Hassan O'Reilly was another City Hotel resident with a British connection. His father was Irish, his mother Lebanese. This melancholy figure, bony-faced, with deep-sunk intense eyes, haunted the hotel's balcony, misfortune radiating off him like heat off a tarmac road. I found him there on several evenings, staring into the dust-laden dusk, at the darkening sea, visible between two buildings. He always wore a soiled white vest.

Hassan was a man waiting. He told me he had been involved in a business deal which had gone wrong. His partners had fled with his investment and the profits. 'To Ghana, probably.' But he knew they would return one day, and he would be there 'waiting to get what's mine'.

He said he had expected to make thousands of dollars from the deal. Now that it had gone wrong he was broke. He wanted to 'borrow some leones'. I gave him several hundred leones. Not an altogether altruistic act: it helped to lighten the burden caused by wads of soiled leones that amounted to less than fifty pounds.

He did not volunteer what the failed business deal had involved. And I did not ask, preferring to speculate that he might be a failed diamond smuggler. It seemed, somehow, more romantic and Greene-like.

Mr Fereira also didn't ask too many questions about his guests. 'Who cares? They come, they pay, they go.'

The City Hotel's main rival in the colonial days as a hang-out for the colonialist was the Hill Station Club, the social haunt of gin-soaked melancholy Civil Servants and their lonely, unloved wives. It is above the city, and from its terrace is a view of hills as enchanting and tranquil as any I'd seen in Jamaica.

The interior of the Hill Station Club shared the City Hotel's air of lost comfort, of faded grace, of decayed elegance. The snooker tables were torn and patched, their balls as grimy as a football on a rainy day match, their cues untipped and crooked. The only British faces now were hidden in the shadows of the past. On one occasion I watched a group of Lebanese men play, their thick gold watches glittering under the table lamp. On another day I met a 'Big Man', whose mountainous stomach and sweaty face betrayed that he had – as they say in West Africa – 'chopped well, well'. We got to talking about Sierra Leonean politics and he sighed for the 'good old days' of 'Pa' Stevens. He asked if I'd seen the late President's house. He was neither the first nor the last Sierra Leonean to ask me that question. I could hardly not notice 'Pa' Stevens' architectural legacy: a vast villa which, from the sonorous height of an isolated hill, shouts at the Atlantic Ocean; a vain, bombastic symbol of sudden wealth.

The 'Big Man', like other Sierra Leoneans, admired it, but unlike some others did not speculate on how President 'Pa' Stevens, once a trade-union leader, acquired the wealth to build it. Those who did pointed to one source: diamonds. The fall of Greene's policeman anti-hero, Scobie, was caused partly by his entanglement with diamonds smugglers. Diamonds have been the ruin of many a man here and they may yet destroy the myth of 'Pa' Stevens.

Today's European diamond smugglers are unlikely to be found in the ancient quarters of Freetown. The city has grown since the forties, spread southward towards Cape Sierra. Here, a small but flourishing tourist trade centres around Lumley Beach, where open-walled Lebanese restaurants sell pitta bread, olives and humus against the background of an Atlantic Ocean becalmed on the Freetown shoreline. Above the beach are three modern hotels, which seemed to be the new incarnation of Greene's shady world.

I stayed in the Bintumani, named after a local king, and in its breakfast room became acquainted with a young Frenchman, Jacques. Often unshaven, he slouched in every morning with a swift furtive survey of the room. He was handsome and had the casual, self-assured air of the French in Africa.

Jacques had been in Sierra Leone for five years. What he did was never clear. 'Import-export.' 'People think it's easy to make money out of these African countries,' he said over breakfast one morning. 'It's not. You can if you learn the African's patience. A guy will buy some machinery in France. He thinks he has a buyer here. He will come with the machinery expecting to be paid on delivery. But he has to wait. Six months later he's still waiting. The African, he might genuinely want the machinery, but he knows if he can outwait the European, the European will leave, and he will get the machinery free.' Jacques, too, seemed like a man waiting. Some afternoons, having returned to the hotel for a break, I would notice him sitting by the poolside, unshaven, reading a book.

The Colonel, a mysterious figure: quiet, bald-headed, ramrod straight, a direct gaze. He agreed with Jacques. The Colonel was American and he had been coming in and out of Sierra Leone for only two years. He had fought in Vietnam and built up an engineering company and was now trying to win export orders. The Colonel and I were to have lunch, but it never happened. He cancelled.

I was compensated for that disappointment by an encounter with Steve Omerod in the hotel bar one night. Large and flabby,

he drank whisky as if it was soda. After he'd described himself
as a Kenyan I'd explained what had brought me to Africa, and
he called me a 'Black Englishman'. To which I instantly replied,
'Then you must be a White African.' And we laughed ironically
at these once unimaginable juxtapositions of identities.

Steve Omerod was in fact more of a White African than I
could ever be a Black Englishman. He was a third-generation
Kenyan. His father's roots were in Lancashire, his mother's in
Scotland. A few years after his parents' death, he sold his
inherited interest in a Highland farm and left Kenya. He bought
a Japanese Landcruiser and, with a friend, drove across the
continent in an adventure which sounded like an experience Jack
Kerouac would have envied.

That journey ended in Nigeria, where he married a Nigerian.
'Three children. But those Nigerian women. Too much *wahala*
[aggravation]. I bought her and the children a house and left.'
Now he imported farm machinery and boasted that he worked
three days a week. 'From Thursday to Sunday I am on my
yacht. Some fishing. Visiting the islands. Love Banana Island.
You should come. Get some girls, some whisky.'

Though I could not take it up, I was flattered by the invitation
– though I also sensed some over-anxiety to prove his Africanness – because he had told me that those island visits had
become rare of late. 'I've seen this country down,' Omerod
said. 'But I've never seen it as low as this. There's no petrol.
To get it you have to bribe. Serious bribing. I ask myself why
should I pay fifty thousand leones for four gallons of petrol. So
we don't sail too far now.'

I asked him whether he ever visited Britain.

'I go there regularly, to London mostly. My main suppliers
are there. But I don't like the place. I am an African. I don't
feel comfortable with Europeans. I was in London a few months
ago and stayed in Earls Court. I was lonely and missing home.
One day I met some African guys and I invited them back to
the hotel. We spent the whole weekend drinking. We had a wild
time in that hotel.'

As we spoke the bar had slowly filled with the girls who
nightly descended on the Bintumani. Omerod seemed to know

many of them. When one girl, who walked like a burlesque whore, passed by, he called out: 'The hookers done come-o.' She came back and placed a fleshy arm around his shoulders.

'You want *juku-juku*, Steve, Baby,' she said with a drawl through lips thick and glistening with lipstick.

'You give me free,' Steve teased.

'How I go chop if I give you free *juku-juku*?' she said. 'Buy me a drink.'

He bought her a Coke, and she slinked off to join the other girls. (Some of these girls, I was told by the barman a few nights later, were married, had families, and by day worked in respectable jobs. But the ever-decreasing value of the leone forced them to haunt hotel bars. Their husbands understood that 'everybody must dreg to survive', he said ruefully. He himself was a partner in a taxi, which he drove for part of the day before coming to do his night shift at the hotel.)

We were later joined by a thin, bearded German who introduced himself in a heavily accented voice as 'Ziggy, short for Zigfried'.

Ziggy was a diamond prospector still searching for the 'big one'. He had passed over gold in search of diamonds. Though he hadn't found a 'motherlore', Ziggy remained optimistic that his boat would one day come in. He had been in Sierra Leone for over twenty years and had no immediate plans to leave. 'The French are proud. America is big. And Sierra Leone is sweet,' he said with a gummy, lascivious chuckle, glancing at the birds of the night.

Steve Omerod's rough charm lost its attraction for me after Ziggy's arrival. The two men encouraged each other in a conversation which became obsessively lewd as the night wore on. I left them by the bar and strolled towards my room, brooding on why I'd earlier felt an affinity with Omerod, on Europeans in Africa, past and present; and on the ill-fated Scobie, who by now seemed like more than a fictitious creation of Graham Greene's imagination.

SIX

FREETOWN TO CONAKRY

The heat and decay of Freetown had such an enervating effect on me in the first few days that I looked forward to leaving. But on the morning we set off for Conakry, driving through streets thronged with hopeful school children, worried office workers, jolly market women and furtive street boys, I felt the melancholy of departure.

Despite its dissolute atmosphere – maybe that played a part too – the city had charmed me. The beach, which I visited at the end of working days, had left me with some especially fond memories. I'd scrubbed my body with its fine-grained sand; watched a magnificent sunset over the Atlantic against a backdrop of Bob Marley's lamentation for 'Kaya' – 'Got to have Kaya now 'cause the rain is falling'; listened, around midnight, to the anger of the darkened ocean. So terrible, so tragic, so timeless.

The journey had also acquired a new tone in Freetown. The daily business of conducting interviews, which could involve five-hour periods with Noah, had not generated any further acrimony. It helped that he had become calmer, less nervously energetic, and, it seemed to me, more reflective; and I had also begun to appreciate his efficiency. We had developed an amiable working relationship, and I seldom asked myself, 'What the hell am I doing travelling around Africa with a White guy?' as I'd done at least thrice a day in Monrovia. When, for whatever reason, the question now stole into my mind, I was inclined to smile crookedly, like someone who possessed an amusing personal secret. Moreover, I'd created opportunities to wander about alone by extending my day late into the night, which had been tiring, but rewarding. These changes made me less conscious of Noah; and I had begun to feel at ease with the journey. As we sped out of Freetown, I was not bothered by the knowledge that we were heading into Francophone Africa, where Noah's fluency in French would be crucial. Freetown had helped to restore the balance between the professional broadcaster and my spirit of Africa, which had, at the outset, rebelled at the prospect of this journey.

After Kissi, Freetown ended abruptly and the road twisted upwards. For a while we ran parallel with the lusciously green riverine plain of Bunce River; passed Waterloo, and then climbed up through the Occra Hills. There were few vehicles on the road, only the odd truck laden with vegetables, bare-chested men seated on top, the sun coruscating off their white smiles. On flat stretches we raced through palm farms, and the golden fronds and barks of the trees seemed to tint the air gold.

The driver, Idris, was a laconic Mende who handled the vehicle, a Japanese Landcruiser, with admirable skill. Indeed, there were moments when his concentration on the road, his posture behind the wheel, powerfully suggested a fusion of man and machine. Long, muscular arms outstretched, immense hands gripping the steering-wheel, he conveyed a stillness which inspired confidence. He was accompanied by a mate. And like the Monrovia to Freetown drivers, they seldom spoke.

I'd just begun to applaud the quality of the road, when it changed dramatically. The jeep bounced on to an ochre-coloured track and the windows had to be turned up to keep out the dust. This laterite track was interrupted by a brief stretch of tarmac and resumed as we entered a dreamlike landscape. It started with a pile of wrecked, rusting cars and vans, which appeared to have collapsed, irrecoverably, at a point where the dirt track and tarmac met. Then came a long, straight, dusty stretch, wide as a New York avenue. The land was flat and almost treeless. Beside the road, for half a mile, a fire had left behind thin, black trees which, as they flashed by, seemed like strange beings who had perished in the flames.

Miles further on we came to Port Loko, a town of untarmacked roads, a town where the dust lay thick on roofs, cars and leaves, like snow. Even the people's darkness seemed tinted rusty red. Beyond Port Loko we crossed a river that rushed over huge smooth boulders. Among the boulders, dwarfed by their immensity, a man washed himself, lathered from head to toe. A spectre.

On the other side of the wide, swift-flowing Great Scarcies, we stopped for a rest at a village, where the Landcruiser was almost as tall as the houses. Waiting for my companions beside the river below a breadfruit tree, I felt a deep love for this land of my ancestors, a love of its size and beauty and mystery.

Then we were back on the road and, it seemed, in no time at the Sierra Leone–Guinea border. Our driver, Idris, knew the Sierra Leonean customs officers here and we were dealt with quickly. Approaching the Guinea entry point, my first sight was of a red, gold and green flag dancing in the warm breeze.

While my companions handled the entry formalities, I went to stand under the shade of a tree. I had not been standing there long when an elderly man brought a bench from a hut, signalled for me to sit, and offered me a piece of kola-nut. He muttered something in French and when I showed incomprehension switched to another language which I didn't understand either. I tried the little Hausa I knew, and he responded with, 'Sannu da Zuwa' (greetings at your coming), and I said, 'Na Gode', which almost exhausted my stock of Hausa words. Sensing the communication gap, he wandered off behind the wooden building.

On the other side of the border, in Guinea, the road improved fantastically. It looked new, and we sped towards Conakry through a landscape that became greener by the mile. To the north a never-ending low hill ran parallel to the road.

Conakry began with an industrial estate of furniture manufacturers and bottling plants. A wide, busy avenue full of traffic led towards the sea and the heart of the city. For a moment I thought we were going away from the city because we began passing tiny, rough houses, like adobes, and women sat on dusty sidewalks cooking, while children played around them.

These houses gave way to an open space bordered by nim trees, and barefooted boys played football in their shade on the dry grassland.

The Novotel Conakry, our destination, was a little further down the road. We had not made reservations and this turned out to be a problem. The hotel was full. While Noah explored possibilities with a pretty Ethiopian lady, the assistant manager, I went with Idris to find Conakry's only other international hotel. But I had no luck there, or at the only recommended local hotel.

Returning to the Novotel, with thoughts of spending a muscle-cramping night in the Landcruiser, I learnt that the hotel did after all have some rooms. Two Arab gentlemen were due to leave that evening. Saved.

We said goodbye to Idris and his mate – they planned to spend the night with friends in Conakry. I bought some postcards and wrote them out and sent them to dear friends. I did this beside a swimming-pool overrun with Europeans and overflowing with the sound of French accents. They looked like businessmen, engineers and technicians. Children and women were amongst them. A quite different crowd from the adventurers I'd sensed amongst the guests at the Bintumani in Freetown.

Restless, but relieved that I wouldn't have to pass the night in the jeep, I wandered around the hotel grounds. Beyond the pool, I noticed a large gathering of people at the seafront, over-shadowed by the red, gold and green of the Guinean flag. I decided to wander down there. My stroll took me past rusting Second-World-War cannons pointing out to sea. Young soldiers stood beside the cannons. It seemed incredible that these decrepit weapons were expected to have any effect on hostile forces. Further along, the skeleton of an iron boat lay on its side, like the exhumed bones of a long-extinct creature preserved by the sea-salt. Between guns and beached boat, on charcoal-grey sand, teams of ragged boys played football, some with papier mâché balls. The liveliest game used a plastic one, the size of a tennis ball. It was full of excitement and drew a small crowd of spectators.

The much larger crowd I'd seen from the hotel, the gathering under the fluttering flag at the water's edge, consisted of fishermen and buyers, mostly women. I walked among them and recognised faces that I had seen in London, Jamaica, New York, though never with such a uniformity of colour. Fish were being sold from nets or in baskets, like oranges or bananas. The smell was overpowering, and fish scales stuck to people's clothes and cheeks.

Wandering through this market I was aware that some people noticed my foreignness. It was evident in my clothes, my trainers – still white, despite the dust – my almost new T-shirt, my pressed trousers. Perhaps my strangeness announced itself too in the way I walked and looked around. I felt I was being watched, but not with hostility. Curiosity. And I felt completely safe, wandering among these strangers with the faces of friends and relatives.

A child fell and started crying; his mother scooped him up, while balancing on her head an enamel bowl of fish.

The people's clothes were rough and simple. To the side of the fish market, a man sold second-hand European-style clothes; a woman sold gigantic grilled fish that attracted flies, which she listlessly brushed away. Battered taxis, Russian and Japanese cars, came and went, as if in slow motion.

Walking back to the hotel, I left a zone soaked in the odour of raw fish for one drenched in the stench of raw sewage – the hotel dumped its waste into the ocean and the tide was coming in.

It had been a short walk and by the time I reached the hotel dusk had fallen and night followed swiftly, as it does in Africa. Later that evening, I watched a party of Guineans arrive for a reception in the garden. They were dressed in smart French suits, cravats included, or resplendent gowns that stirred the air as they passed.

The next morning I met Dialla. I'd been standing in front of the hotel, when he approached me. 'Taxi, Monsieur,' he said. 'Allow me to show you Conakry.' He had read my mind because I had been wondering how to see the city in the few hours I had to spare. In fact I did not need two hours to see Conakry. I'd seen most of it the previous evening. The Hotel Novotel was a few minutes' walk from the Parliament building, and the main shopping area and the village-like streets where women sat cooking in the open air. Rich and poor here, powerful and powerless seemed to live cheek by jowl. Fishermen hung their nets on the lampposts outside the Parliament building, and dried squares of tiny silver fish were laid out on the pavement.

When I realised a car wasn't needed to see Conakry, I persuaded Dialla to walk with me. His English was better than my French and he wanted to improve it. He said he had travelled to fifteen African countries and lived and worked in Ghana, Nigeria and Liberia. He liked Monrovia, where he had worked on the docks, because 'there is plenty money. Guinea too poor. No work.' In Ghana he had sold oranges and cigarettes. Nigeria, he said, had been 'very tough'. He had almost starved to death. 'Nigeria very tribalist,' he said.

We had coffee and croissants in an air-conditioned café furnished in art-deco style. An oasis of Parisian elegance. From the café we wandered back in the direction of the hotel. It was midday and the streets were busy, but not that busy. Lebanese cloth merchants leaned in the doorways of their shops and their faces wore the solemn, ruminative expression of traders who had known many rainy days in the sunshine. We walked along the narrow streets of low, simple houses. Bob Marley wailed from a radio. A child bawled somewhere.

A Sierra Leonean had said to me, 'If you think we're poor wait until you see Conakry.' I had not taken him seriously, but strolling with Dialla through Conakry, that remark now rang with truth. But Conakry's poverty was of a different nature from that of Freetown. Sierra Leone was part of the free world and remained poor. Guinea had recently emerged from over two decades of political and economic isolation from the West. It didn't even have enough hotels for foreign visitors. Their absence gave Conakry an air of innocence, unlike Freetown, where it was possible to imagine all kinds of shady deals happening.

Conakry reminded me of Dar es Salaam, Tanzania's capital. The two cities seemed to share the same peaceful almost rustic atmosphere. Recalling that a Tanzanian I'd met had said to me that he preferred to be poor than exploited, respected than

wealthy, I asked Dialla which was more important to him.
Wealth or respect?

'Respect,' he said, without hesitation. 'But it is good to have
both,' he added swiftly.

We passed the Parliament again and strolled down wider
streets lined with dwarf mango trees and modern houses,
inspired in their design by Islamic architecture. Dialla explained
that these houses had been built for the ministers and senior
Civil Servants. They were not grand houses, but coming so
quickly after the adobe-like houses they seemed almost Gothic.

'Why is Guinea so poor?' I asked Dialla.

'Sékou Touré. Oppression. Conté is better.'

Abdullahi Conté succeeded Sékou Touré, who ruled Guinea
for over twenty-six years and died in a hospital in Cleveland,
Ohio in 1984. Dialla's belief that Touré had caused Conakry's
poverty came as a radical surprise to me. For much of the
sixties and seventies in the West, among Africa-oriented
Blacks, Sékou Touré was the only surviving independence
leader spoken of in the same breath as Kwame Nkrumah, the
man who led Ghana to independence from Britain in 1957. His
defiant remark made to General Charles de Gaulle was often
seen on liberation posters: 'We prefer freedom in poverty to
riches in slavery'. He was a hero of the African world.

And when Stokely Carmichael, the Trinidadian-born American Black power leader, fled the United States to avoid criminal
charges, he found refuge in Guinea. Here, he changed his name
to Kwame Touré, further bolstering Sékou Touré's image as a
pan-African in Nkrumah's mould. The reverence accorded
Touré by outsiders in need of heroes, unfamiliar with the
internal politics of Guinea, was, it seemed, misplaced.

The cab-driver Dialla was not the only Guinean who spoke of
the late leader as an encumbrance to development. Immediately
after parting with Dialla, I interviewed Portus Diallou. A foreign
minister under Sékou Touré, he is now Chairman of the Guinea
Bar Association, attorney of law and a member of the Consti-
tutional Drafting Committee. This body was created after Sékou
Touré's death in 1984.

Like many post-independence politicians, Diallou was

imprisoned in the Sékou Touré years. He spoke with a quiet anger about his ordeal: 'The Guinean political prisoner never knew on what charge he had been condemned. Consequently, he knew neither at what date he would get out of prison nor indeed if he would ever get out at all. He lived with uncertainty and with perpetual anguish but also with the constant hope of liberation.'

In 1958 the then French President Charles de Gaulle initiated a referendum to determine which of the French colonies in Africa wanted membership of a newly reorganised French Community. Twenty million colonial subjects in West Africa were asked to vote 'Yes or No' on this issue. An affirmative vote would mean close economic and cultural ties with France. A negative vote, de Gaulle stressed, was a vote for total independence, a complete severance of economic and cultural links. Forbidding terms. They implied that French links with West Africa were solely beneficial to the Africans. Only one country voted 'No': Guinea.

The French reaction was full of spite and venom. The entire French administration was withdrawn. Departing Civil Servants destroyed files and even pulled out the telephones and took them back to France. Sékou Touré, the nationalist leader who had inspired his people to vote 'No', after witnessing this enraged French flight asked: 'How can a mother abandon her children?' However, the mother did not simply walk away. This was the era of the cold war, an age when pro-independence acts could easily be interpreted as pro-Communist acts. Guinea became to France in Africa what Cuba was to the United States in the Americas.

The French plotted and schemed to topple Sékou Touré – the young Communist as de Gaulle called him. Slowly, inexorably, Sékou Touré transformed Guinea into a police state. He saw plots to oust him everywhere; and in the solitude of his power 'The Lion of Africa', as he was called, devoured his nation.

I asked Mr Diallou whether there were features specific to Guinean culture which predetermined the result of the referendum. However, the language barrier, I suspected, made this question sound rather naïve.

He replied: 'I return the question to you: Why would Guinea not choose independence? When you are a slave, they ask you, do you like to be free, or to remain in slavery? We had an advanced culture and our own states (the Fuluni and Susu peoples of Guinea had their own polities before the arrival of the Europeans) and could not just accept to remain in slavery since we were asked to choose.'

I wondered whether Guineans regretted taking the independent path. Was there, perhaps, envy of the countries which had remained within the French community?

'No. I don't think we envy those countries,' he said. 'It was the people who voted for their independence and they meant it. What all of us really regret is the way Sékou Touré governed the country. It wasn't just a dictatorship. It was more than that. It was totalitarianism; we entered the one-party system. From sixty to eighty-four we had so many plots. But all of them were just in the mind, in the mad mind of Sékou Touré. He centralised all the power. He had his own police, his own militia educated in Cuba. It was the same structure as in East European countries.'

'Yet the one-party system remains popular in Africa,' I remarked.

'Because it is a very easy way of governing. You inject your ideas to the people and your ideas come back to you. But it is the worst way. After the charismatic leader, what happens to the one-party system? Ours was the strongest in Africa. After the death of Sékou Touré, three days after his burial, it disappeared completely.'

I suggested that perhaps Guinea had benefited from its independence in the sense of developing greater national pride than its neighbours.

Mr Diallou agreed, and said, 'In the early years national pride flourished. But with the method of government of Sékou Touré, there was a disintegration of the unity. The way Sékou Touré governed. It was an ethnical way. More than that. It was a family government, like the one we observe in Romania with Ceauşescu.'

He expressed optimism that Guinea would make a successful transition to that multi-partyism. But Guinea's future, Diallou stressed, lay down the pan-African path. He saw no future in the many tiny states of West Africa (one of France's legacies to the region in contrast to Britain's experiment with federalism in West Africa and elsewhere on the continent), and looked forward to the day when they would pool their experiences and resources to create regional unity as a step towards that pan-African goal.

The Guinean lawyer believed the historical ties with France could not be severed easily; nor, in fact, was that desirable. 'It is better to improve relations. There will come a day when we will have to thank them [the French] for helping to create some kind of political unity. One day, maybe sooner than later, we will achieve what President Senghor called *"Civilisation de universal"*.'

That evening, after speaking to Portus Diallou, I boarded a plane for the Senegalese capital, Dakar, leaving behind a Guinea still recovering, six years after his death, from Sékou Touré's despotic reign. But I was undecided on how much Sékou Touré's record resulted from his own weaknesses, as opposed to France's policy toward Guinea after the 1958 referendum. How much the abandoned child had erred in response to punishment from a mother who felt she had been scorned.

SEVEN

IN SEARCH OF THE AFRICAN
PERSONALITY

'A stick can float for a long time in the water but it will never become a crocodile' (Wolof proverb).

Dakar was only an hour's flight from Conakry but the real distance between these two capital cities was immeasurable. If Conakry was the ravaged face of a precocious child abandoned and driven to acts of self-mutilation by a vengeful mother, then Dakar was the pampered face of a patient sibling who, while aspiring to independence, expressed its aspirations in more acceptable terms, winning the indulgence of *la mère*. For I was instantly struck by the Europeanness of Dakar.

This most westerly of sub-Saharan cities abounds with flashy office-blocks, solemn old buildings, tree-lined avenues, narrow lanes, spacious squares, pâtisseries, clothes and jewellery boutiques, and pavement cafés. And the French are highly visible. They own and run many of the stores and cafés, and at the end of a working day, scores of Frenchmen can be seen leaving ministry buildings, where they work as *conseillers techniques*. The result is a city with an unusually strong Parisian atmosphere. This Parisian feel is combined with the quite different air of an Africa close to Islam: tall men in resplendent gowns uncoiling from Peugeot cars; squatting beggars with arms outstretched, chanting monotonously in Arabic outside pavement cafés; kaftan-wearing pedlars selling apples.

The ubiquity of the French in post-colonial Dakar is partly

rooted in history. The French settled in Senegal in the seventeenth century, first in Saint-Louis, further north on the coast, and then Dakar, which became the Capital of France's West-African empire. Independent Senegal is a senior member of a Francophone West African community that includes Ivory Coast, Burkina Faso, Chad, Central African Republic, Guinea, Benin, Togo, Gabon and Cameroon. Most of these states are small and ruled by autocrats of unusual longevity. France has more troops in Africa than any other Western power, reflecting the extent of its interest in the region.

In contrast, British settlers preferred the cooler climes of East and southern Africa to the humid coastline and semi-deserts of Britain's West African colonies. Britain seems to have regarded these colonies as a necessary but unenjoyable – indeed, dangerous – part of its 'civilising mission'. An attitude expressed in a song from the slave-trading days: 'Beware and take care the bight of Benin. There's one that comes out for forty goes in.' Compared to the French, the British took flight from West Africa after independence.

British and French settlers also brought to Africa radically different social attitudes. Shortly after arriving in this Senegalese city I spent a pleasant and enlightening evening in a pavement café drinking *petit café* with a Malawian, Thandikum. He had lived in Dakar for many years and confessed to being an obsessive observer of the French in Africa. 'The French had a less Calvinist view of life in the colonies,' Thandikum told me, 'They didn't wear khaki. They dressed up. Africa was a long summer holiday for them. The Anglophones were more formal. It's the same difference between Paris and London.'

Having spent most of his life in Malawi, Thandikum found 'the relations between the French and the Africans less strained. The French keep mistresses. You can read a diary of an Englishman in Africa without there being any mention of sex. The French have less taboos about things like that. As someone from southern Africa, I think the form of racism here doesn't take the same form as among the British. Apartheid, after all, is in the south.'

The everyday differences between French and British

settlers observed by the Malawian were underpinned by a fundamental difference between French and British colonial policies. Britain was concerned principally with the economic exploitation of Africa and tampered with Africa's indigenous political structures only where they impeded commerce. Culture – education, religion, language – was left to the missionaries. French colonialism on the other hand, though no less inspired by the profit motive, went a step further: it also tried to make of the African a Frenchman.

And it was here in Senegal that France pursued its assimilationist policy with the greatest vigour. This policy was summed up by a German explorer, Heinrich Barth: '. . . that France above all should understand this great mission which the Lord has entrusted to her . . . by sending missions composed of men of clear courage and integrity and of superior intelligence . . . to serve as intermediaries and interpreters between these more or less savage people on the one hand and the civilisation and institutions of Europe on the other . . .'

These ideals, of course, were tempered by the realities of colonial administration. Efforts to destroy traditional institutions, for instance, were not wholly successful, especially where Islam had a stronghold. But to the extent that the French succeeded, Senegal became less marked by ethnic divisions than other West African countries. Reducing the power of the chiefs – the repositories of tribal custom – weakened tribal allegiancies and identities, and simultaneously accelerated the growth of a Senegalese national identity. Consequently, Senegal is not as riven by ethnic rivalry as many other West African states.

However, Senegal's vaunted national unity is not seamless. The Senegalese are worried about Casamance. This southern region, divided from the rest of Senegal by The Gambia, has given birth to a separatist movement – *Mouvement des Forces Démocratiques de Casamance*. There have been skirmishes between the separatists and government troops despatched from Dakar.

The troubles in Casamance represent more than the threat of another African civil war. They also expose the weakness,

in geographical spread and emotional grip, of the idea and sentiment of belonging to a nation in independent Africa. In the rural
areas national identity still has yet to fully triumph over ethnic
and regional allegiances, which are no respecters of the national
boundaries drawn by colonial administrators and maintained by
their heirs in distant capital cities.

Capital cities tend to be more like symbols of an aspiration
to nationhood in Africa. A traveller can never help noticing how
abruptly the concrete and metal of the city ends and the open
space of the countryside begins. Dakar is no exception. I spent
most of a Sunday outside Dakar, driving through a flat, arid
land; past sand-dunes, baobab trees, small villages of sandy
streets; across a landscape which sometimes appeared to have
remained untouched by the modern. Returning to Dakar, suddenly entering the city, was like driving into a mirage.

Some days later I spoke to a sociologist at the Cheikh Anta
Diop University in Dakar, who both confirmed and challenged
my impression. Fatou Sow took offence at my description of
Dakar as an 'unAfrican-looking city'. She replied: 'Foreigners
say Dakar is not Africa. It looks like Paris. But such visitors
speak only to the élite. It has to be remembered that less than
twenty per cent of people here speak French. Even less speak
really good French. That means that after roughly three hundred years of French penetration only twenty per cent. If you
leave the capital then there is no more French influence. It's
just an impression.

'Even if the French language is present in administration and
education, at the level of culture, once you peel off this layer
of French influence, you find something else. Typical African,
Wolof, or Mandinka or *Jola* culture. And the French have little
to do with that. The French influence is a strong layer, but it
is also thin.'

I then remarked that it wasn't that I hadn't noticed non-
French influence, but what I had seen seemed to be mostly
Islamic.

'Islamic culture is very important. There have been Muslims
in the northern part of the country for centuries. We have been
a vector for Islamisation from the north to the south. Around

eighty-five per cent here are Muslims. People are very religious, then Islamic. But the influence of Islam stops when it comes to what you really do think, what you believe in.

'African culture expresses itself in all spheres of life. We have had many influences. But they are just influences. We are Africans. We practise African culture. Even if it's tinted with French connotation, Islamic connotation, British connotation. If a French or Briton spends fifty years of their life in Africa, people never say they are African. They are British. Nobody denies them their Britishness. Why do we have to be denied our Africanity?'

How that Africanity was expressed beneath the appearance of French and Islamic culture escaped me. So I asked Fatou Sow what, for example, was the Wolof death ritual and what was specifically African about it?

She described a ritual which began with the Muslim influence and then progressed to one that she regarded as typically Wolof: '. . . women talk together and speak of the deceased, then we have a sort of socialisation. People come and sit around the widow. That's over eight days. I think it's typically African, when someone dies it's an occasion for the community to come together and have a celebration.'

I observed that in the Caribbean the death ritual included something similar. But the Bible, rather than the Koran, would be read or quoted and the occasion was known as nine-nights; I should also have said that her description of the mourners' attitude to the dead sounded similar to the one I had heard from Bishop George Brown in Liberia.

*   *   *

Fatou Sow's forceful defence of Dakar's underlying Africanness appealed to a concern of mine. Having travelled across the African continent, through North America and the Caribbean, I have wondered whether Africans, and African descendants

share something more in common than their universal second-
class status, their status as victims of White racism. Walking
through Brixton, Harlem, Lagos, Kingston, Dar es Salaam, I
have sensed a commonality in the music, the rhythm of walkers,
in the food; some intangible quality which makes me feel like a
traveller amongst people who, however dispersed, however
different their shades, share a common cultural spirit. In other
words, is there an essential African identity independent of
racial oppression?

There was a time when an answer to this question was as
important to the Senegalese as the notion of democracy was to
the authors of the American constitution.

Dakar is closely associated with two of the big ideas generated by Africa's independence struggle: Negritude and pan-
Africanism. Although these ideas are related, the weight of
emphasis placed on them by nationalists varied between the
French and British colonies, reflecting differences in the colonial
experience of the two territories.

Pan-Africanism, a political idea, was championed mainly, but
not solely, by West Africans from the British colonies. The
English-speaking West Africans gave little thought to Negritude. Their attitude to it was, after independence, summed up
by Wole Soyinka: 'A tiger does not need to declare its tigritude,
it pounces.'

In Senegal the idea of Negritude was accorded great importance, elaborated and refined. French colonialism assumed that
Africa was, at best, a *tabula rasa* on which to systematically
write French culture and, at worst, a barbaric place fortunate
to have been blessed with the fruits of French civilisation. The
independence struggle in Senegal was inseparable from a vibrant intellectual and cultural attack on that assumption. Senegalese intellectuals and artists quarrelled both with the French
and themselves, with the result that rhetoric, poetry, fiction
and historical studies flourished.

Léopold Senghor, Senegal's first president (from 1960–
1980), was the leading light of the Negritude movement. He
defined Negritude as: '. . . the whole of the values, social and
political – which characterise Black people. It is essentially

instinctive reason . . . it is of the impression, reason that is seized. It is expressed by the emotions through an abandonment of self . . . the sense of communion, the gift of the imagination, the gift of rhythm, these are the traits of Negritude.' The implication of Senghor's definition was distilled in a controversial statement: 'Reason is Hellenic and emotion is African.'

The Negritude movement was neither novel nor restricted to the African continent. It belonged to a tradition of African thought which could be traced back to at least as far as Edward Wilmot Blyden, who emphasised spirituality as the defining feature of Africans. It was also heavily influenced by African-American poets like Langston Hughes, Countée Cullen and the Jamaican writer Claude McKay. Physically removed from Africa, their ethnic identities destroyed by slavery, leaving them only with a racial identity, the descendants of Africans in the West had long been asking, 'What is the essence of the black man?' The answers, some of which identified and celebrated 'emotion', would wend their way back to Africa.

Senghor's own link to this tradition was forged in France, where he lived from 1928 until the 1950s. As a philosophy student in the Sorbonne he came into contact with other Africans and, crucially, African descendants from the French Caribbean islands. Among the latter was the Martiniquan Aimé Césaire, whose *Return to My Native Land* is a classic of the Negritude position and world literature:

'Those who invented neither gunpowder nor compass,
Those who never vanquished steam nor electricity,
Those who explored neither seas nor sky,
But who know in its uttermost corners the landscape of
pain . . .'

We did not invent because we can feel, we dance, the Senghor and the Negritude writers seemed to declare. This kind of thinking about the essential differences between Africans and Europeans is still found today. An African-American academic addressing an audience in London raised the roof with laughter when he quipped: 'It's an indisputable fact that we dance better than White folk.'

Senghor's attempt to identify the essence of the African, though influenced by the Africans in the diaspora, did not always find acceptance there. For example, Ralph Ellison, author of *Invisible Man*, has argued: '. . . The American Negro people is North American in origin and has evolved under specifically American conditions; climatic, nutritional, historical, political and social. It takes its characters from the experience of American slavery and the struggle for, and the achievement of, emancipation; from the dynamics of American race and caste discrimination, and from living in a highly industrialised and highly mobile society . . . Its spiritual outlook is basically Protestant, its system of kinship is Western . . .

'Culturally this people represents one of the many sub-cultures which make up that great amalgam of European and native American cultures which is the culture of the United States. This "American Negro Culture" is expressed in a body of folklore, in the musical forms of the spirituals and the blues and jazz; an idiomatic version of American speech (especially in the southern United States); a cuisine, a body of dance forms and even dramaturgy which is generally unrecognised as such because still tied to the more folkish Negro churches.

'It is not culture which binds the peoples who are of partially African origin now scattered throughout the world,' Ellison continues, 'but an identity of passions. We share a hatred for the alienation forced upon us by Europeans during the process of colonisation and empire, and we are bound by our common suffering more than by our pigmentation. But even this identification is shared by most non-white peoples, and while it has political value of great potency, its cultural value is almost nil.' (Ralph Ellison, *Shadow and Act*.)

Ellison would be hard-pressed to defend his entire argument against the vast and growing body of research, from within the Americas, documenting the survival of African cultures through slavery to the present day. None the less, Ellison's implicit rejection of the notion of a common African culture which transcends time and space is not entirely groundless. After all, the

African descendants who returned to the continent to create Liberia and Sierra Leone remain, even today, distinct ethnic groups.

The poetic and philosophical discourse of Negritude owed much to the times in which it flourished. Senghor was in Paris during a period marked by the rise of European fascism, which also attempted to define the European. Senghor and Césaire and the others were, in part, reacting to that fascist project. The Europeans had defined themselves as rational beings, the bearers of a civilisation rooted in rational scientific thought, as distinguished from the primitivism of other peoples, especially the African.

The philosophers and poets of Negritude did not challenge the European perception of the African. Rather they celebrated the very qualities which the colonisers held in contempt. In so doing they implicitly sanctioned the classification of the 'races' formulated by nineteenth-century European thinkers like Gobineau, a father of modern racism.

That the idea of Negritude brushed so close to such dangerous formulations partly accounts for its relative unimportance today. The waning popularity of Léopold Senghor, once the high priest of the movement, has also contributed. He resigned as Senegal's President in 1980. At the time of his resignation it was widely rumoured that he had been advised to step down in the interest of national stability, or risk a coup. He became the first nationalist leader to peacefully relinquish power, handing over to Abdou Diouf, his political godson. Now he spends his time between Dakar and France, where he is the first African member of the Académie française.

Furthermore, Senghor himself has retracted some of his early ideas: 'I admit that as Negro students in the years nineteen thirty to nineteen forty we were only an obstruction. I admit that we were racialist: we were intoxicated by the banner of Negritude. At that time no intercourse was possible with Europeans. But since then, because it led to deadlock by imposing cold war between races and continents, between man and man, we decided upon reflection to make an extra effort. Today we have accomplished this – the results of European decolonisation have contributed to it – we have left behind us the period of denial to embark with you upon the period of construction.'

That construction, in progress since independence in 1960, has created a city which has the peace of Dar es Salaam and the Parisian love of culture and ideas. I have sat late into the night on a concrete bench in Independence Square, watching the red, gold and green of Senegal's flag flutter in the breeze of the Atlantic; contemplating the meaning of being an African.

*   *   *

In post-independent Senegal some of the Negritude writers became political leaders and mandarins.

Cheikh Hamidou Kane is the author of *Ambiguous Adventure*, a classic of Negritude fiction about a young man's rites of passage from Islamic to French culture. Kane is a former diplomat, minister of industry and minister of planning. I spoke to him in his Dakar office. Slim and youthful-looking – he was sixty-one – there was about him an air of calm urbanity.

I had noticed that Dakar did not appear to have suffered the flood of migrants from the countryside characteristic of other African capitals, like Nairobi or Lagos and asked him why.

He proudly declared that Dakar is a very well-designed city, better designed than, say, Lagos. But for the past decade the effects of the Sahel drought had placed Dakar under great pressure. Before that there was seasonal migration to Dakar; the migrants would return to their farms at the start of the rainy season. Now they stayed in Dakar, with many choosing emigration to places as far-flung as Zaïre, Paris and New York (I have in fact seen and heard French-speaking West African car mechanics working on battered vehicles on a Harlem street corner, their faces ashen in the cold). He thanked God that the rainy season had become more reliable, keeping people on the land.

It was Kane's belief that Negritude had 'played its historical role'. This was helped by the fact that Léopold Senghor 'felt it necessary to focus on the return of the Black man to his culture. With Léon Damas, Aimé Césaire and Birago Diop, he wanted to demonstrate to the West, to the Europeans, that the Black men who they had enslaved, who they had colonised, were a people who had their own culture, their own identity. They felt the need to demonstrate that to the Europeans and at the same time to demonstrate it to themselves and to their people, to people like them who had been to Western schools. Because the people, the Senegalese people who had not been abroad, or been to Western schools, did not need to be reminded of their culture or their origin. The French were assimilationists. The British were different; in their colonies they lived apart.'

I suggested that perhaps while the British have a strong sense of historical achievement, they attached less importance to culture and cultural identity; they did not seek to codify their culture and then export it.

'Yes, the French, together with the other Latin races, Italian, Spanish and so on, are universal-minded. Also the Catholics are universalists. While the Saxons, the Germans, the British, are more intertribal-minded.'

How did he personally rebel against the French attempt to make him a Frenchman?

'That rebellion came late for me and for most of my friends. It came after I had been in the French school for more than ten years. Only when I started university level that I started feeling opposition to what it had made of me. I felt that they had been denying my culture. They didn't think that I could have my own traditional religion, my own way of feeling. It was at that time that I began feeling that the family into which I was born had its own values which were better than what I understood were the values practised in the French family. That was the whole content of my *"L'aventure ambiguë"*.'

Cheikh Hamidou Kane recalled giving a speech, as a student of Dakar University, which criticised the French hypocrisy, which denied Africans the vote. 'They claimed that the problem was because the French-born had documentary proof of their place of birth and age and therefore could be registered to vote;

but the Africans did not. But I observed that the Africans' lack
of documentary proof did not prevent them from levying taxes.'

But he emphasised, with a quiet sense of indignation, that
that political revolt was secondary to the intellectual and cultural
revolt he experienced.

Yet Senegal remains a nation intensely dependent on France,
arousing resentment on the part of the post-independent generation. How did he respond to the anger of the younger generation?

'The younger generation in Senegal feels impatient not necessarily against the remaining French influence, but because they
don't have the jobs they would like to have; and this resentment
has been fuelled in many of our countries by revolutionary ideol-
ogies, like Marxism.

'But the need to revolt against French influence is less important than the need to assert our own African culture. To assert
it against French and Western influence, as well as against
Marxist influence. It is easier to understand that the Western
influence is a bad one, than it is to recognise that the Eastern
influence is a bad one. Because the Western influence is neo-
colonial. So people can revolt against that. While the influence
of Marxism had appeared until perestroika to be the only revolutionary way.'

However, he conceded that his generation, those who took
Senegal into independence, were not entirely blameless. 'Our
greatest failure was to accept independence outside a federation
of Francophone West African states.' In the years leading to
independence, France frustrated the federal ambitions of nationalist leaders who recognised that small weak states could be
easily manipulated. For example, Ivory Coast and Upper Volta
(now Burkina Faso), which had been administered as one unit
under colonial rule, were separated.

I was enjoying Monsieur Kane's deft intellectual footwork in
relation to the younger generation's fondness for Marxism. So
I asked him whether the rather intimate French–Senegalese
relationship owed anything to a shared fondness for rhetoric,
for words, for ideas. I'd noticed that taxi-drivers and traders
seemed to enjoy arguing, and they did so with a uniquely

engaging playfulness. But Monsieur Kane somewhat side-stepped the question, observing that foreigners other than the French had long lived in Senegal, where the word *'Karangga'*, meaning hospitality, was taken seriously.

As Cheikh Hamidou Kane belonged to the generation which had taken Africa into independence, he was ideally placed to identify the continent's pressing needs. When I put this question to him, he straightened himself and answered with formal dignity: 'Greater African unity, a scientific and technological cadre and the assertion of African culture.'

*   *   *

The importance of cultural matters to the Senegalese was brought home to me one day on a visit to Sandanga Market, in the heart of Dakar. Walking through this market – French, Arabic, Wolof and other languages exploding around me – I heard the following song about Cheikh Anta Diop: 'From Senegal to the gate of Africa, passing through the pyramids to Egypt, the cradle of modern civilisation, no man's wisdom exceeds that of Cheikh Anta Diop, battling Eurocentric ideas, like those pretending that reason is Hellenic, Cheikh Anta Diop spent his whole life refuting ideas derogatory to the black skin.'

There aren't many countries where a nuclear physicist, historian and political activist would be remembered in a pop song. Like the French, the Senegalese celebrate their intellectuals. And they do so in song. When the musician and *griot*, Elhadj N'diaye, sings of Diop, he is performing an ancient function – remembering and spreading word of his people's great achievement.

Cheikh Anta Diop was until his death a fierce intellectual and political opponent of Léopold Senghor. Diop and Senghor were equally concerned with the search for an African personality. But while Senghor's was a poetic quest, Diop called upon history, linguistics and archaeology. He vehemently rejected the

Senghorian notion that reason was Hellenic and emotion African. And in support of that rejection pointed to the scientific
and technological achievements of ancient Egypt as an example
of an African civilisation. Furthermore, he attempted to demonstrate that his own ethnic group, the Wolofs, were direct
descendants of the ancient Egyptians. The African had not only
invented things, Diop sought to demonstrate, his civilisation had
provided the bases for European civilisation.

In an interview with Carlos Moore in 1967, Diop said: 'When
we talk about personality, meaning the personality of collective
groups, we can only mean a cultural personality. And what is
the basis of the cultural personality of a people, African or
otherwise, if not a historical, psychic and linguistic self-
consciousness. These three elements are the constituent
elements of a people's cultural personality or identity. They
are not static factors conditioned by man's social and physical
environment . . . My approach has clarified what is called the
particular sensibility of the Black man, or Black soul. I have
tried to determine the nature of the Black particularity in history
and to ascertain the way in which the "Black soul" or Black
sensibility has influenced the material existence and creativity
of Black peoples by using the structures evolved by ancient
Black societies as a basis . . . The way I saw it at the beginning
was that Africa's soul had been stolen and could only be
retrieved through a scientific approach.'

Diop was a passionate pan-Africanist and saw his work as a
contribution to the achievement of pan-African unity. This total
political and cultural commitment to Africa brought him into
conflict with the more moderate Senghor. Diop wanted Wolof,
instead of French, as Senegal's national language, a reduction
in French influence in Senegal's affairs, and stronger links with
other African countries.

Diop's research on African history has spawned a whole
school of African historians, and his works have been extremely
influential amongst African-American historians. Here in Senegal he remains a highly respected figure and is regarded in some
circles as the country's greatest pan-Africanist.

However, like Senghor's romantic Negritude, Diop's

scientific Negritude has its critics within Senegal. Among them is Abdullahi Bathally, a British-trained historian and political activist. Bathally is a great admirer of Cheikh Anta Diop but locates himself in a generation which feels a need to transcend Diop.

'. . . in the nineteen-fifties when he wrote his major work, the question was an ideological battle between the colonial historical discourse and the historical discourse the African intelligentsia had to put forward against that colonial discourse. Since colonialism was dismissing any role for the African in the building of human civilisation, his work has contributed very much; has played, let us say, a role of stimulant in the political struggles in the fifties and in the early sixties.

'But at the same time in the post-colonial era, of course, the new generation had a different relationship to history. They started questioning not only the colonial discourse but also, to a certain extent, the nationalist discourse, in the sense that the nationalist discourse tended to put too much emphasis on the factors of greatness in African history, and not attempt to demonstrate the cause of failure and the shortcomings in our history.

'It is not enough to talk about the greatness of the past, but also what made it possible for the same Africans to be as dictatorial as the colonial masters, as exploitative as the former colonial masters.'

It is understandable that the search for the African personality, once all-important to Senegal's intelligentsia, should become less significant as the nation confronts the reality of independence. However, that early preoccupation has created an invaluable space in Dakar – a city of intellectual and cultural vitality – where Africans can address cultural issues, perilously neglected elsewhere on the continent, as an intrinsic part of the quest for a viable independence.

EIGHT

A DAY ON GORÉE

'Gee, ain't that beautiful,' a middle-aged female voice gushed with the affectionate enthusiasm of a grandmother seeing her first grandchild.

I was standing on the seventh floor of a Dakar hotel, gazing at the Atlantic Ocean. It was mid-morning and sunlight danced on the ocean's smooth turquoise surface, creating a play of light and darkness that was indeed enchanting. An open boat filled with men streaked across the water with a flock of gulls in trail.

I had been waiting for the elevator and found distraction in that picturesque scene framed by the window.

I turned and faced a woman wearing a T-shirt – on which was emblazoned the legend: 'Black History Month' – and green chequered slacks. An American; an African-American.

She came from Philadelphia and was in Dakar with a party of visiting African-Americans. This was, for her, 'the trip of a lifetime – to see Mother Africa'.

After that encounter, I discovered African-Americans everywhere in the hotel. They ranged from teenagers to young adults and grey-haired folk, some of whom looked as though they were nearing retirement. They came from different parts of the United States, from the east coast to the Midwest, some from obscure little towns. Their days were filled with visits to historic sites in Senegal. The height of this African pilgrimage was a day in Jaffour, the Gambian village to which Alex Haley, the author of *Roots*, claimed to have traced his African ancestry.

One afternoon I fell into conversation with some of the younger pilgrims. They all came from Indiana and had an earnestness about them which I had previously only associated with dedicated churchgoers. A young woman, who said she was a mechanical engineer, was the most responsive to my questioning conversation.

It was her first visit to Africa and, true to the promise of a friend who had visited the previous year, the modernity and Westernness of Dakar suited her fine. Why had she come?

'To know more about my history and Africa. At home the only thing we hear about Africa are the coups and famines; and South Africa. When my friend told me about Dakar, it really spaced me out, you know.'

'What have you learned about your history?'

'About the slave trade and the civilisations that were here before. You know, there are some things that White folks don't want you to know, like the fact that we got a history that isn't all about slavery, like the fact that we had great empires in Africa. Knowledge is power. Maybe they scared we gonna take inspiration from knowing 'bout our past and really badmouth them.'

An elderly gentleman seated nearby interjected and said the 'White folks' he worked with were really excited about his visit and asked him to bring back lots of photographs.

I said it seemed to me that most White folks didn't know and were not too concerned about their own past; so maybe there wasn't a conspiracy to deny Africans in the diaspora historical self-knowledge.

The young woman disagreed vehemently, saying, 'When I was in college I visited Europe and all my White friends were really enthusiastic and gung-ho about the Tower of London and all that stuff. You know, they got it. They got access to it. Now we African-Americans are gonna get some of that stuff. We got roots.'

African-Americans? I asked when and why she had started describing herself in such terms; what happened to 'Black-American or Afro-American.'

'That's what we are, have always been, Americans of African

descent; Africans in America. But we were scared to call ourselves that for a long time 'cause White folks might be upset.
But, you know, brother Marcus Garvey and brother Malcolm
and brother Farrakhan, all those brothers, they teach us to say
what we are: Africans. We knows we're American. Now we
getting to know the African in us.'

'Could you live here, in Africa?'

'I could live in a city like Dakar, or near it. Gotta have my
running water and electricity. Constant, you know.'

I was enjoying my conversation with her: she had innocence,
honesty and enthusiasm. I would have wanted to see her living
in Africa ten years on; to see how the ardours of an African
existence aged her. But I suspected that she, like me, would
always return to the West, to our minority status there; but
strengthened and emboldened by an African sojourn; a return
to the source.

We then got to talking about the explosion of African-
American female writers; which appeared, I suggested, to
coincide or even contribute to the decline of their male counterparts. Her own view was that the women had been neglected
and now was their turn. We agreed that after the anger of the
men – the Wrights and the Ellisons and the Baldwins – the
spiritual pain of the women, the heart of the race, needed to be
voiced.

These African-American pilgrims were helped in their search
for 'Roots' by a team of Africans, mostly Gambians, who acted
as guides. Jerry was one. With his round steel-rimmed glasses,
blue jeans and rucksack, he looked like a student and spoke
impeccable English. Jerry had been working as a guide for three
years. He liked the 'Black-Americans' and implied that he found
their fascination with Africa flattering: 'We are so poor and yet
they are curious about us.' He had four children and each day
spent four hours travelling to and from the hotel to do his job.

Was I interested in joining his party to The Gambia? 'Banjul
is beautiful and quiet.' Apparently Princess Anne was visiting
Banjul and the occasion promised to be full of pageantry,
African-style. I ruefully declined as my Dakar schedule had
already been drawn up.

It was Jerry who introduced me to Mohammed Africa. This stocky African-American, born in Harlem, had lived in Dakar for nine years and changed his name when he decided to stay permanently. Had I seen him on the street, I would not have guessed that he was anything but a Senegalese, perhaps a trader of some kind. He wore local dress, a rather grubby white kaftan.

Mr Africa ran a travel agency, specialising in tours for African-Americans. He had plans to build a wax museum of African heroes in Dakar – Marcus Garvey, Martin Luther King, Malcolm X, Lumumba. It was a familiar pantheon. He asked me for Madame Tussaud's address as he wanted to begin exploring the idea further. I admired his courage. A wax museum in tropical Africa presupposed regular electricity.

Mr Africa was concerned about the future of Africans. 'Wherever we are in the world we're at the bottom,' he said.

I suggested that there were historical reasons for that fact.

'We can't keep on blaming it on history,' he said with passion. 'Now that Eastern Europe is free, Africa will be neglected. Development funds will go there.'

I said that may not be a bad thing, as much development money had been stolen anyway.

He did not disagree, but in turn suggested that the lessening interest of the Europeans could be replaced by Japanese imperialism. 'They'll take over if we're not careful. When they designed the drum machine, I became scared, man. The drum is ours. They turned it into a machine. We'd better get our shit together or Africa's gonna be colonised again, I am telling you brother.'

Mohammed Africa recommended that I should visit the island of Gorée. Gorée is a former slave fort built by the European traders as a transit camp for the captured slaves awaiting shipment to the New World. A twenty-minute ferry ride from Dakar Harbour, the island's ancient castles of cells with their inglorious memories are amongst the highlights of Senegal's burgeoning back-to-Africa tourist industry. The Senegalese, with African-American assistance, are planning to build a monument to slavery there.

The potential of this industry is not lost on the Senegalese. It already brings in dollars and could bring more. There is even an informal economy developing alongside it. This consists of young men who haunt the streets of Dakar looking for African-American tourists to sting.

To my shame, I was the unwitting victim of such a sting. Outside a Dakar bookshop – where I'd gone to buy French improvement texts – I was approached by a tall, lanky young man. 'Brother,' he whispered, 'you want to buy gold? Senegalese gold. The best in Africa.' Up until then I did not know that Senegal had gold.

I told him, 'No.'

'You from New York, man. Maybe you come from Chicago?'

'London,' I said coldly. I was not in a good mood; something I'd eaten the night before; I hoped to deter him by asserting a sort of frosty Englishness. But this only seemed to heighten his curiosity.

'A brother from London, hey man, welcome to Dakar,' so saying he pressed a lump of metal in my hand. 'Welcome back to Africa, man. Take this. A welcome gift from one Black man to another.'

With metal in my hand, I was suddenly and fleetingly overwhelmed by an indescribable emotion. 'Thank you,' I said. The metal was heavy and for a brief moment I might even have believed it was gold.

'Brother,' he said, 'I have three children, I am an artist. In three days, my youngest has to be christened. I have no money to buy food for my relatives. Maybe you can give me something small.'

'I thought you were giving this to me free,' I said peevishly, thrusting the metal back at him.

'I am, brother. It's yours,' he said, refusing to take it back. 'But maybe you can give me small something. Not for the gold. For my children.'

Anxious to be on my way, I hurriedly pulled a note out of my pocket and gave it to him. He thanked me and bowed and retreated and was gone in an instant. I later discovered that I had given him almost ten pounds, and even later found out that

the metal was brass. A Dakar sting. I had to admire the art of
it.

I had read about Gorée and had vaguely entertained a desire
to visit it. But I could not envisage visiting a former slave fort
for the first time in my life with a White person. There was a
background to this reluctance. In 1979 I made my first visit to
Africa, to Nigeria. My host, a Nigerian who had been brought
up in London, was married to an Englishwoman. I was and
remain fond of the couple.

One day we all went to Badagry, a town outside Lagos and
a former slaving point. The chains are still there, thick rusting
metal, indelibly stained with their bloody memories. Shoeless
little boys earn pocket-money by showing them to visitors.
Seeing and touching the chains was a novel, emotional experience: they stirred sorrow and anger; here, I thought, my unend-
ing and weary journey began. Suddenly a powerful resentment
of the presence of my friend's White wife surged inside me, like
a freak wave. For the remainder of the day I felt a disturbing
hostility towards her.

Hence my reluctance to visit Gorée in the company of another
White person. I had consoled myself with the thought that I
would pass this way again.

Nevertheless, it transpired that an afternoon appointment
was cancelled and when Noah suggested we visit Gorée,
because we had allocated those hours to work, I found it difficult
to refuse. I was an older person, I now reasoned; and, besides,
I'd been told that Gorée had a good beach and swimming
area.

So off to Gorée we went one Dakar Saturday afternoon. A
launch filled with Africans and Europeans. We ate lunch at a
beachside restaurant and I wandered around the terracotta
buildings that surround the Gorée port. A young man, with the
characteristic looming height and slenderness of the Wolof, one
of those guides who always seemed to appear from nowhere,
informed us that the museum cells would be opening shortly;
did we need a guide? I feigned a lack of interest, encouraging
him to concentrate on winning over my companion.

Somehow, though not without design, I became separated

from them as we made our way to the museum. I left the path and walked instead up a steep, rough incline that climaxed in a concrete summit. Dakar, across the ocean, wound its way along the coastline; a long strip of skyscrapers.

From there I continued to the north end of the island, past turrets and disused guns from the Second World War. Gorée's strategic location once made it a military prize; in the Second World War the allied nations guarded it jealously.

I was now several hundred feet above sea level and below the sea crashed and resounded against the rocks. I walked inland and passed turrets that had become the homes of artists and artisans. I was enjoying the walk: the sun above, the copious sweating, the quietness. At the north end of the island I wandered in and out of unused towers that afforded expansive views of the ocean.

I saw him from a distance. He wore a long multi-coloured robe and walked with a stick; he may have had bells on his ankles. We were on the same footpath and had to meet. As he neared I saw that he had dreadlocks. A leather case hung around his neck.

Minutes later we were sitting together in a rocky alcove, the ocean swirling in its ebb and flow over rocks yards from our feet. His name was Abdoulaye Diop and he called himself a spiritual-man and a Mohammadan. From the leather pouch around his neck, he produced a small copper pipe and some brown substance which looked like dried earth. It was Poon – 'to relax', he said. We smoked some together.

Despite his professed religion, Abdoulaye Diop used God, Allah and Jah interchangeably. 'De Babylon man,' Abdoulaye Diop told me, apropos of nothing in particular, 'he rejects his own child.'

'Surely, it is the African who rejected his own child, sold us into slavery,' I replied, with a calm induced by the Poon. I'd often put this question to my African friends. It elicited different answers. The most common, and least honest, upholds the view that Africans had been passive victims of slavery, bought by Europeans who forced slavery on African chiefs. A Nigerian friend had shown shock but gave the matter great thought and finally replied that great tragedies and shame are often surrounded by silence.

Abdoulaye was equally thoughtful and gave me a novel answer: 'The ancestors knew that they could not withstand the military might of the European invaders. The slave trade was the price we paid to avoid total slaughter. But the ancestors knew that the African carries his liberation in his heart. If you have your liberation in your heart no one can imprison or enslave you. The ancestors knew that. They knew that defeat in that battle did not mean defeat for ever. And they were right. The Africans who were taken have won their liberation. Now many, like yourself, are able to return to Africa. Because of that Africa is stronger. But we would be even stronger if we had not forgotten our history.'

A long moment of silence passed between us. The motion of the sea seemed to cast a spell over me. The swirling water, yards away, created a hypnotic rhythm, like a brush repeatedly passing over the taut skin of a drum.

Abdoulaye broke the silence and said: 'Nelson Mandela is free. We should pray.' This second period of silence ended with the spiritual-man chanting in a low, musical voice: 'Lailahailala'.

Then we walked back to the path and went our separate ways; he to his underground bunker, built by Europeans for war, now housing African mystics, like Abdoulaye; and I back to the port.

There I rejoined Noah, who told me, with amusement, of being squashed in a gloomily lit, dank cell with other Europeans listening to an African narrate Gorée's slave history.

NINE

A WALK IN THE FOREST

The flight from Dakar to Douala, from the Sahel region to the rain forest, stopped in Bamako, Abidjan and Cotonou. It was a long, tiring flight, and I disembarked in an irritable and impatient mood, which worsened as I waited in the slow-moving immigration and customs queues. When a customs officer threatened to confiscate a book I had bought in Freetown, my temper snapped and I protested more loudly than good sense dictated. The book's title, *The Origins of the White Race*, aroused suspicion of subversive literature. Fortunately I calmed down enough to explain, with Noah's help, that it was only a collection of folk-tales.

A night's rest cured my tetchiness and made me aware that the journey had reached a potentially dangerous stage: that point marked by a subtle but constant exhaustion which could induce moods that cloud one's judgement.

This was confirmed over breakfast with a disturbingly pale and drawn Noah. His stomach had given him a rough night and he was feeling weak and dehydrated. Amazingly, he still wanted to put in a day's work. I argued that as we were half-way through the journey, and in a comfortable hotel, a brief break now made sense. The alternative was to risk his health and the project by trying to ignore his illness. He reluctantly agreed to take a rest.

While Noah was recovering, I toured Douala in a hired car. There was little to see in this city, which serves as Cameroon's

economic capital. I reached the city limits in several directions
in no time at all. On one occasion, nearing evening, I was
advised to turn back by policemen at a checkpoint on a road
which led to Nigeria. The policemen were friendly and laughed
a lot. On learning of my Jamaican connection, they asked what
had happened to Jimmy Cliff, reggae's first international star. I
related an ancient rumour about his luxurious lifestyle in South
America.

Back at the hotel I met Cameroon's most famous musician,
Manu Dibango. He had been on the same flight – from Dakar.
I had recognised him from his shaven head and dark glasses.
He was in Cameroon with a French television crew. Its
members could be seen lounging about in the hotel lobby, their
strength sapped by the humidity of Douala.

One of Dibango's musicians was a slim, lugubrious young
man who wore a scull-cap over short dreadlocks. He was
called Blaise, and he looked like an encounter between left-
bank radicalism and Rastafarianism. He too was Cameroonian
and this was his first visit back to Cameroon in fifteen years.
He offered to show me Douala's nightlife and we arranged
to meet later.

But at the appointed hour Blaise informed me that he had
been summoned by a relative and would have to fulfil that duty
first. It was not a visit he was looking forward to: 'Zhis is why
I stay in France so long,' he said in a thick French accent. 'In
Africa you don't belong to yourself. Zee family owns you.'

Blaise had written a novel and a collection of short stories.
His real ambition was to be a successful writer. But music took
most of his time. 'My problem is zat I have two wives,' he said
without smiling.

'Why did you leave Cameroon?' I asked.

'To stay alive,' he said cryptically.

He revealed that he had been a student leader and had
incurred the wrath of Ahmadou Ahidjo's Intelligence Service.
They had beaten him to within an inch of his life and imprisoned
him for almost a year. 'Zese African leaders are savages,' he
said bitterly.

I asked whether he had arrived at that conclusion in Paris.

'It is a conclusion I arrived at here, in Cameroon,' he said. 'Zat is why I left.'

'And Europeans are civilised?'

'*Non*,' he replied emphatically, 'zee Europeans are racists. But zey will not beat you because zey, how you say? disagree with your politics. *Non*.'

Blaise's relative lived near the hotel and I offered to drive him there. We would meet back at the hotel later on. I dropped Blaise outside a house that was hidden in the darkness. Its high steel gate and walls reminded me that he had described his relative as a very important man.

Driving back to the hotel along a leafy, dimly lit street, I became uncertain of my bearings and brought the car to a crawling pace. Suddenly, a female figure stepped out of the shadows of a mango and flagged me down. I stopped. I was in fact closer to the hotel than I thought, and the woman was a prostitute. She explained that she could not enter the hotel grounds without a male escort and solicited my help. She said that once we had entered the hotel grounds I was under no obligation to remain with her.

I gave the matter some thought and might have refused had her companion not appeared. She seemed to float out of the darkness towards the car and hovered behind her friend like a timid child. While the first woman was short and plump, her friend was a portrait of beauty. She was tall, straight and had large eyes and slender arms that tapered at wrists adorned with bangles. And there was a ghostly gracefulness about her movement.

I hesitantly agreed to her request. The beautiful girl sat in the back and remained silent on the short ride. Her friend said that she did not speak English. I suspected that even if she had been an English speaker, she would have kept quiet. Her beauty spoke a thousand languages.

They alighted in the hotel car park and I waited for them to disappear before leaving the car. Blaise and I were due to meet at midnight and I had about two hours to kill. I went to my room and attempted to update my diary. But I could not concentrate; words seemed to lose their meaning; an image of the girl floating out of the darkness kept on replaying in my memory.

When I finally abandoned all efforts to write, I went down-stairs. The hotel lobby led on to a terrace of wicker chairs. She sat there, alone; her friend nowhere in sight.

'*Où est votre amie?*' I said, sitting opposite her.

She shrugged her narrow shoulders, which were almost as dark as her black nylon dress. It was a subtle, disdainful shrug, as if I had offended her by daring to enquire of her friend.

'A drink?' I asked.

'*Pour moi?*' she said.

'*Oui.*'

'Coca Cola, *s'il vous plait.*'

When the Coke came she sipped it daintily, holding the glass lightly; her hands, being too bony, were the only visible imper-fection. I learned that her name was Mariam and that she had twins, by a Frenchman whom she had not seen since before their birth. But the language barrier between us did not allow much of a conversation. Initially, she seemed amused; then bored. She kept on looking at her watch.

Blaise arrived presently and I hoped he would join us. But even from afar I could see he was exhausted. None the less, he too showed immediate appreciation of Mariam's beauty. '*Mon Dieu!*' he gasped. 'You foreigners always get the best girls.'

Mariam's smile betrayed her: she did understand English.

Blaise said he needed to rest for an hour; the visit to his relative had left him emotionally drained. 'Too many ghosts to fight,' he muttered.

It was now long past midnight and my passion for exploring Douala's nightlife was on the wane. Blaise was also less keen than he had been earlier in the evening. Instead, he invited me back to his room, where he had a bottle of Chivas Regal.

'What about my friend?' I asked.

'You will pay her for her time and her company?'

I excused myself and walked away with Blaise.

'You mean I'd have to pay just to talk to her?'

'Only if she leaves the hotel lobby.'

'*Pourquoi?*'

'She will have to pay the nightwatchmen. They will not

believe that she went to your room and just talked. They will want money.'

I returned to Mariam and asked her to wait for me, a message Blaise translated on my behalf. In Blaise's room – which was untidy in the extreme – over glasses of duty-free brandy, I jokingly asked Blaise what I should do with Mariam.

'She is beautiful,' he said. 'If I was not tired, I would fight you for her.'

'Fortunately, that would only involve offering her more money than I could,' I said.

Blaise was stretched out on his bed; he was skinny and his eyes were red with tiredness. 'No, no, no,' he said. 'A woman like that will not go with you just for money. She must want you.'

I reminded him that she was a prostitute, somebody forced, probably by poverty, to sell her body.

He disagreed and said, 'To a White man, yes. From you and me she will want something more. We are Black, like her.'

'Not romance?' I laughed mockingly.

'Why not,' he said indignantly, 'and respect, too. Yes respect. She has a right to both.'

I was suddenly ashamed because I felt he was right. My conduct with Mariam had not been disrespectful; but throughout our strained conversation I had not forgotten what she was.

'You must be careful, *mon ami*,' said Blaise. 'Here in Africa, human life is cheap. It can, how you say, er, er, corrupt you. Very, very easily. You see?'

A long moment of silence passed, during which I felt remorseful. Blaise broke the silence by playing a music tape.

'This Africa,' said Blaise. 'Our leaders are savages.'

I was beginning to think that 'savage' was Blaise's favourite word. 'Zey will do anything to stay in power. Look at Doe in Liberia. He makes sacrifices every month. Human sacrifices. He zinks zat by killing a child he will stay in power for ever. Zey all do it.'

'Come on, that's a wild exaggeration,' I said.

'It happens. I know Africa. I am proud to be an African. But we have some bad ways. And our leaders are the worst.'

We talked some more about African politics. Then Blaise, who had been drinking steadily since we entered the room, said he was too tired to chase the night; besides he had to make an early start in the morning. I took that as a cue to leave and told him that I would probably – depending on my companion's health – leave Douala late-morning. We agreed to try and meet four days later in Yaoundé, Cameroon's other major city, where he was due to perform with Manu Dibango. When I reached the door of his room, he said: 'What about the girl? You will take her to your room?'

'I don't know,' I said.

He smiled and said: 'Show her some respect and everything will be all right.'

I made my way back to the lobby in a state of extreme agitation. It had not been my intention to do more than talk to the girl, to feast my eyes on her beauty. Not only was her time money, which I had not thought about, but to possess her, I felt, would ruin the encounter. Yet I did want to see her again.

When I reached downstairs, I saw her standing by the elevator with a Greek-looking man. She averted her eyes and I walked past casually, as if she was a total stranger.

Too agitated to sleep, I went for a drive through Douala. The city streets were near-deserted and on the edge of the city roadside, vendors, their faces illuminated by the light from wood-fires, sold fried fish and roast plantains.

Later that night, from the balcony of my room, I looked out into a dark, dark Douala night, listening to the wall of mysterious sounds, and shame came over me with the thought that not only had I somehow failed a test of humaneness, I had also stepped too close to a precipice, and I felt less confident in my experience of Africa, less the knowing traveller.

*   *   *

The following morning Noah told me he was feeling much better. Rehydration pills he had taken had worked. Around mid-morning we checked out of the hotel and hit the road for Bamenda, a four-hour drive from Douala. The road journey from Freetown to Conakry had given me a taste for the road and I looked forward to the added thrill of driving, as opposed to being driven.

Noah seemed pensive and subdued, physically weaker. But there was also about him a reassuring resolve to move on.

I thought I had a good idea how to exit Douala but I mistakenly entered the port. There were no signs; not even a gate. Rusting containers and mountainous stacks of reddish timber, the ships closer than when I'd passed this way the previous day – all hinted that I might have erred. Security guards stopped us at a gate at the other end. The car was thoroughly searched by a formal but not hostile official.

I stopped again on the edge of Douala to fill the petrol tank. I tried to buy some chewing gum and peanuts from a boy by the roadside. He refused my currency note and seemed not to believe that it was genuine currency. He wanted coins. When I produced the coins the young trader smiled happily, and jingled the metal with confidence. Central Douala was less than twenty minutes away, but already the countryside had begun.

Back on the road, I asked Noah how he felt. 'Rotten,' he said. 'But I'll be all right.' I said I would drive for the day and he should rest; we had enough hours of daylight to reach our destination before dark. He solemnly agreed, and I thought I sensed a wounded pride, a disappointment in himself, as though he felt his illness made him a lesser man. Strangely, I liked him like this: tainted by an unwarranted sense of failure, a little frail. We had been travelling together for almost a month and we had inevitably argued and quarrelled. We had started, after all, as relative strangers. So I welcomed the chance to feel towards him, not pity, he was too young and proud for that, but an odd tenderness.

Passing vehicles became fewer and because it was a smooth road my mind wandered back over the journey so far. I recalled to myself the incident with the Minister of Information in Monrovia and smiled. It now seemed comical and I hoped that my ailing producer would also one day remember it with amusement. Less amusing was the bitter quarrel which followed it: I had neither felt such humiliation nor such genuine anger in years. I had been mulling over that aspect of the incident since it happened.

Now I remembered a snippet of a conversation I'd had many years before with a St Lucian woman recently returned from a long stay in the Caribbean. She had said she felt closer to herself on the island, more sensitive to her emotions because she did not have to bottle them up, whether joy or anger or sorrow, as life in Britain seemed to require. I couldn't remember my response but I thought now that I had not really understood her. I wondered how often I had either failed to recognise my own emotions, or suppressed them for the sake of survival or ambition; ignored subtle and obvious slights in order to avoid a fuss. Wondered whether my feelings, hardened like a calloused hand in Britain, were revived in Africa. Then I thought the landscape of emotions and its ocean of memories belonged to another country and I was too old or too ill-equipped to start exploring those remote, dark, deep regions; or too afraid of what demons I might discover lurking there . . .

My attention was suddenly brought back to the road as we entered a valley, flanked on the west by a low, undulating mountain range, like a reclining body, and farmland nestled in its curvatures. At points a peak rose from the range's slumber, suddenly shooting skywards, its summit enshrouded by clouds. A marvellous landscape for escape and fantasy, I thought . . .

'How about some music, Noah?' I said with an affected cheerfulness.

We had been on the road for over an hour and Noah's appearance had visibly improved. He spoke briefly about his early childhood in the Canadian Rockies, which had left him with a love of mountains. And I could see he was looking forward to this stage of the journey, where we would visit a mountain village.

I wasn't as enthusiastic about our destination and my much milder anticipation of what lay ahead bothered me now. The countryside simply held no great excitement for me, yet I could clearly remember a happy time during my childhood in Jamaica when I roamed across open fields and rose early in dew-soaked mornings to collect avocado pears that had fallen to the ground overnight, when night brought tales of magic and ghosts, and eerie sounds. Inseparable from those memories were lucid images of my great-grandmother, Nana. My parents left me and my brothers with her while they joined the great gold and honey rush to London. I recalled her now, on that Cameroon road, as being tall and erect. Someone who endured life with a grim resolve, and organised it around the need to keep death from knocking at her door until she invited him, as he had done with her husband. Dwelling in trees and under rocks, in streams and pools, were good and bad spirits to whom she regularly offered propitiatory gifts to ensure her a healthy and long life. With Nana walking stiffly across my memory, I realised that there was a period in my life when the countryside meant magic, rituals of entry into a world beyond the ordinary eye; and that I had lost that world. Lost it on the voyage to London, lost it in a great childhood disruption, the effects of which continued to haunt my adult life.

But I did not welcome this invading sense of loss. So I thought instead of my love of cities. Give me cities, I mused, give me New York's mountains of skyscrapers, its broad avenues and car horns playing mechanical jazz. Give me Kingston where the market women, their legs splayed, with piles of mangoes and bananas at their feet, sit all day hopefully watching the daily tide of humanity ebb and flow. Give me a London park on an early summer morning when the leaves of horsechestnut trees are still translucent. Give me the city and I'll take the countryside – the park – within it.

Then it occurred to me that perhaps my indifference to the countryside had something to do with my own peculiar brand of Englishness, which is circumscribed by the boundaries of London. Beyond that city's limits is another country where, in my most extreme moments of insecurity and paranoia, I imagine all the people and forces hostile to my presence on their island reside . . .

We had a light lunch in a restaurant opposite an agricultural station. A near-accident preceded lunch. Parking the car, I scared a motorcyclist by reversing and braking too close to him. He was unharmed but clearly upset. I placated him with a drink of his choice, a large whisky, which he consumed with great panache on the restaurant's narrow verandah watched enviously by two other diners. The restaurateur, needless to say, welcomed my generosity.

This minor incident betrayed my melting urban confidence. Back in the city I would have been considerably less appeasing: I would have cursed his careless driving, or riding.

The road from here on snaked through the mountains and hills, winding, rising and falling along the contours of the landscape. It demanded a constant alertness that enhanced one's sense of being alive. Overtaking slower vehicles, lorries laden with timbers, minibuses packed with passengers, was an exercise requiring precision, anticipation and, at times, courage. It was mostly single-laned and the many bends forced one to sit on the tail of the vehicle ahead waiting for a suitable moment to nip briskly into the other lane, overtake, and return quickly. When attempting this move on a hill, only a low gear would ensure success. Then the engine revved and you could feel the strain in the car, which generated an uncertainty that only subsided once the move had been executed, replaced by calm exhilaration. The summit of the incline nearing, you prepared for a new sensation, going down hill.

We had been collecting music tapes throughout the journey and now took the opportunity to listen to some. One of the many we played was a moody elegiac song by Youssou N'Dor, which complemented the magical air of the surrounding mountains. Noah became talkative again for a while. He spoke of his Catholic mother and Jewish father, implied that they had found liberation from the constraints of their respective religious backgrounds in the Canadian mountains.

As he spoke and revealed more about himself, my sense of affinity with him grew. We were children of this tumultuous age, the eve of the millennium, physically displaced and culturally dislocated, confronting life without the certainty of religion, the security of tribal ties, the illusory belongingness of nationalism. And I felt hopeful for the next century.

We stopped to buy some bananas from women on the roadside. They sat beneath thatched shades. Behind them was a sheer drop to a flat, dry valley of stunted trees and brown grass. Signs that we were nearing the savannah.

Within an hour we were in Bafoussam, a large town that marks the beginning of the savannah. Here the town's roads were dusty and long views obscured by a haze. From a first-floor café in the town centre, I watched heavy-limbed Cameroonians make their way to and from a market opposite. One woman wore a smock, made from colourful African cloth, inspired in its design by the clothes of German Puritans, a legacy of the Lutheran missionaries who came with the short-lived German colonisation of Cameroon. Other traces of that history were evident in the sturdy, pragmatic outlines of stone churches on hill-tops.

On the outskirts of our destination for the day, we stopped again to watch the sun set in the far end of a natural corridor created by intersecting mountains. It gently disappeared behind a hazy, cloud-streaked sky, its light like that of a bulb swaddled in muslin. Some children, their skin ashen with the dust, inured to this wondrous sight, watched us instead with avid curiosity.

By the time we had found our hotel, dusk had fallen. Named 'Skyline', it stands above Bamenda, a large town that stretches through an immense valley. The lights were coming on there; they appeared suddenly on the valley floor, which soon looked like a swarm of fireflies. With the swiftly nearing darkness, music rose up; reminding me that it was a Friday night.

The sight of Bamenda, of electric lights and buildings, helped to assuage my nerves exposed by a mixture of tiredness and the distressing absence of the feel and sound of my natural habitat, the city. But when the hotel manager allocated me room number thirteen, my dormant superstition violently awakened, triggering my immediate and uncompromising protest. I was given another room. From its balcony, my calm restored, I watched night fall over Bamenda.

Bamenda, being sited in north-west Cameroon, is close to

Nigeria. In fact, it is in a region once considered a part of Nigeria. In the preparations for independence, a referendum returned in favour of belonging to Cameroon. The resultant division, between Anglophone and Francophone Cameroon, is as wide, though not as deep, as the ravines between the country's innumerable mountains.

In the sonorous darkness of the people, one begins to feel Nigeria from Bamenda. The Nigeria of Gongola, a state in the north-east of Nigeria, the other side of the mountains. My own connection with that behemoth of Africa was in the north, the savannah, where I had worked for two years in a university.

Early next morning we set off again; this time I was a passenger. Oku was supposedly two hours' drive away. But we were warned that it all depended on how well the car performed on a road that had tested and failed sturdier vehicles than ours. I soon saw why. It was another dirt track. The car seemed to slide forward as if on ice, leaving behind a thick trail of dust. Country folk who walked along the road over long distances were covered in the dust. By the time they came into view it was too late to slow down, which would have stirred less dust. But it would have added a day to the journey. Taxis and buses hurtled past on the flat, even stretches and only slowed down where the track failed completely.

Nevertheless, I was enjoying the ride, the landscape of fields and hillsides, of a land that did not so much undulate at times as dance away into the distance.

At a particularly slow point on the road, a group of people waved us down. They carried boxes and cases and wanted a ride. We agreed to take the person with the lightest baggage. This was a woman in her twenties. She sat in the back and said little; her English was poor, her French non-existent. She spoke one of Cameroon's two hundred-plus languages.

After an hour's driving we stopped in Kumbo, where we ate a late breakfast in a wooden shack run by two boys. Its walls were plastered with pictures from Western colour magazines. Breakfast was coffee sweetened with Nestlé's milk, and sweet white bread sandwiching avocado pear. On the edge of Kumbo was another relic of the German presence in the form of an

indomitable-looking stone church. Our passenger alighted
shortly after Kumbo. Then for a while the road became treach-
erously steep, one incline so precipitous that even in first gear
the car almost stalled.

Nearing Oku, a tyre blew, its outer wall ripped by the stones
in the road. We changed it quickly. In Oku the land seemed to
close in a little, became less expansive. It was all farmland.
Terraces for planting encircled hillocks; in some places these
small hills were bare, the land exhausted. Oku had been
described to me as a forest village, but so far there were no
signs of a forest, only a dying land.

After some enquiry we found the house where we planned to
stay until Sunday afternoon. Our hosts were John and Heather
Parrot, a British couple, with a baby boy called Mungo, after
the eighteenth-century Scottish explorer. They ran the Killum
Mountain project, part of a British Aid Scheme, which sought
to arrest the destruction of the forest.

From John I learned that all the land we had driven through
in the last half an hour of the journey was once covered in forest.
In the space of thirty years the forest had receded rapidly with
the demand for food from Cameroon's growing urban population. New types of farmers had sprung up, overnight investors
looking for quick returns from cash crops like coffee. The high
price of coffee on the international market was a special bane,
as it brought in more get-rich-quick farmers. These trends,
combined with the traditional practice of using the forest for
firewood, augured an ecological disaster, which, he believed,
could only be averted by restricting access to the forest, and
developing a new relationship to it.

The couple arranged a guide to take us on a walk through the
forest. But as we were strangers, permission was required
from the local chief, the Fon. His palace was a few hundred
yards down the road. Our guide Alfred – muscular with a large
head and deep-set eyes – led us there.

Coincidentally, on that day a Mfon, the Chief's council, was
in progress. So, we first had to pay our respects to the Mfon,
and only with their permission could we proceed to see the
Fon. The Mfon was being held in a capacious mud hut. Only

men were allowed in and all entrants, without exception, were obliged to carry a weapon, a knife or a sword. A long dagger in a worn leather scabbard was hung around my neck.

Inside the cool dark hut men sat on rough wooden benches talking. Our entrance caused silence, then a commotion. The chairman called the assembly to order. He explained that the Mfon met once every eight days and all members were required to attend. He himself had travelled a great distance to be there. While he spoke he held a twisted stick. This was his symbol of authority and members of the assembly could only speak when he'd handed them the stick. Speaking without the stick was an offence punishable by a fine; persistent offenders were expelled from the Mfon.

The chairman's explanation gave me an opportunity to gain some insight into the difference between traditional and modern rule. Were traditional rulers more representative than their modern counterparts, less prone to dictatorial rule? How easily, for instance, could an errant chief be removed; what checks and balances affected his rule?

The chairman translated my questions to the Mfon and they laughed heartily. There was some consultation; then he replied: 'The Mfon can and has removed a chief. We have procedures. But not everybody can become a chief. A chief must come from a chiefly family. But even so, he can be removed.'

A few men, who presumably understood English, nodded in agreement and the members of the Mfon talked amongst themselves excitedly for a while. Then palm wine was brought out and I drank mine from a small gourd, its taste rancid and sweet. The chairman then began chanting and the men rose and the drummers stood over their instruments, some chest-high. There followed for ten minutes heavy drumming punctuated by the clashing of steel against steel as each man withdrew his sword or knife and repeatedly crossed it with his neighbour's. A slow, barely audible chanting rose gradually until it reached a feverish pitch and all the voices became one. Even I felt fused with the spirit of the Mfon, in that dark, damp hut on the edge of a mountain forest somewhere in Cameroon.

Slightly intoxicated by the palm wine and the ritual, I listened with a growing sense of unreality, as of a dream, to the chairman bestow membership of the Mfon on us. He said its members were all over the world, and when we met a Cameroonian we should enquire whether he belonged to the Mfon. If so, he would be obliged to treat us with hospitality and friendliness.

The meeting with the Fon was anti-climactic after that. We were taken to his palace, an enormous mud building. A small, shrunken old man emerged from behind a curtain and sat in a chair that must have been built for a person ten times his size. He gazed at us with lachrymose eyes set in a wrinkled face that betrayed neither indifference nor curiosity. The chairman of the Mfon represented us. We were then called forward to introduce ourselves. The Fon said nothing, he merely nodded his tiny head and seconds later we were outside.

It was late afternoon by the time we reached the forest. Here the air cooled perceptibly and the light dimmed but for pockets of almost epiphanous light that streamed through the canopy. Unseen birds sang from the roof of the forest and occasionally I heard the fluttering of wings as they took flight. We passed beehives and concealed traps for birds and animals, and now and then Alfred, the guide, pointed to a tree whose raw trunk revealed the actions of forest thieves. We stopped abruptly when Alfred commanded us to listen. And when my ears had sifted through the many sounds of the forests, the birds, the rush of water over stones, I heard a mechanical whine. 'The forest is dying,' Alfred said solemnly. Somewhere in the distance, somebody was destroying a tree.

In his gentle voice, at times pained, Alfred explained that in the old days, when he was a boy and before, there were rules for using the forest. Certain trees were revered, others could only be used for specific purposes – he pointed to a tree used only for making the marimba (a wooden xylophone). Respect for the forest was inculcated from infancy with tales of evil spirits, and later on a boy became a man by spending nights in the forest, learning how to survive in it, how to avoid releasing the evil spirits, how to win the support of the good spirits. But now nobody feared the forest. They only saw money in the trees. Alfred said he hoped the White man would teach the people of Oku how to respect the forest again.

We could not wander too far into the forest as night neared. So we returned to Oku, to John and Heather's house. Here we ate dinner while dusk fell; night followed quickly on its heels.

John and Heather were keen to find out about events back in Britain. I tried to satisfy their curiosity but Britain seemed not only physically distant, but also like some unimaginable land that belonged to another time. Noah was a better reporter of events there.

The routines of the city, established in my teens, were not easily forgotten: it was a Saturday night and I wanted to do Saturday-night things. But dinner on a Saturday evening followed by conversation, exhausted my hosts' repertoire. 'The men here go to the bar down the road, get drunk, if they can afford it, then go home and sleep,' John informed me. A discouraging piece of information, which I ignored. I later used the pretext of needing cigarettes to go for a walk.

The Oku night was without electricity and unlike any other night I could remember experiencing. A viscous darkness made me feel as though I were wading through liquid. The stars seemed so close that all I had to do was reach up and touch them. Voices came from the night but there were no faces, no bodies. Occasionally someone passed but I only knew this after the event. The shop I had been directed to had no cigarettes. The shopkeeper, his face illuminated by a kerosene lamp, directed me to the local bar. His teenage daughter walked a part of the way with me in silence. When we arrived at the bar, its windows lit by the light of kerosene lamps, she turned back. A few young men sat inside drinking stout. My presence, my foreignness, caused whispers.

I bought some cigarettes and a stout beer and wandered out on to the porch, to luxuriate in this incredible night. I had been standing there for some time when one of the drinkers came out to join me. He wore a jumper, the Oku night being cool. His features were hidden in the darkness, revealing themselves in shadowy fragments.

We exchanged names and then I said: 'What do you guys do on a Saturday night?'

'We drink. Maybe we go to Kumbo. Plenty happen in Kumbo.'

'Do you ever drive back at night?'

'Yes. But not too much. The road is bad. Soon light will come to Oku. And we won't have to drive on road. The road is too bad, very much too bad.'

'Why, now?'

'You see, we suffer too much in this countryside. The people in Bamenda, they enjoy. Douala and Yaoundé they enjoy very much. But there is more: the government fear an invasion. We are close to Nigeria. If the road is bad, the Nigerians will not reach far.'

'Are you serious? Why would Nigeria want to invade Cameroon?' As I said this I remembered an incident from 1981: Cameroonian border troops killed six Nigerian soldiers. For months afterwards the Nigerian Press whipped up anti-Cameroon feelings of great ferocity, demanding immediate retributive action by the government.

'That is how it is,' he said simply.

I asked about his family and he told me he was not married but lived in his father's compound and worked on the farm and that he would always live in Oku because the city was too far and too big. I bought him a beer and told him about my family and where I lived. Then I asked him to tell me a story. This is a paraphrase:

A young man journeying in search of his destiny came upon a forest. He entered along a path and walked a great distance until nightfall, when he sought shelter in a cave. There he encountered an old man, who welcomed him and offered him food. When the young man had eaten, he took from his bag the clay cup he always travelled with. The old man remarked that the young man was not motivated by the prospects of wealth, though it would surely come his way. 'How do you know this?' the young man asked. 'Because of the many things a cup can be made from you use one that is made of the earth.' The young man laughed and said someone with a gold cup was hardly likely to be walking alone in a forest. The old man replied: 'You came here by a path cut by many travellers before. Do not presume to know who they might have been. You have entered the cave and you may continue your journey through the cave. Beyond here is a wall, to go further you must scale that wall.' When the young man saw the wall, he could see little point in attempting to scale it. The old man told him: 'You will travel paths travelled by others but because you are lazy you will never climb the walls that lead to glory.'

The house had been locked for the night when I returned. Having to knock and wait reminded me of my antipathy to staying in other people's houses. But as it was only for this one night I did not feel too badly.

Noah woke me at some absurd hour, around six a.m. and I was filled with a deep hatred of him, which only subsided after I'd washed my face in the fresh cold water, finally vanishing with breakfast and my first sight of the morning sky. A grey cloudy canvas.

Alfred came shortly and we drove back to the forest. A soothing stillness reigned here; not even the leaves rustled. A mellifluous music came from the tree-tops, like Satchmo in a playful mood, and Alfred explained that it was the sound of the fon, the bird from whom the chief takes his title. This endangered bird has rich scarlet feathers, which are used to denote status among the Oku people.

On the previous walk we had crossed the forest, now we climbed it, following well-trodden paths; sometimes digressing along overgrown paths. Alfred, who carried a machete, would shout back when turning on to a long-unused path. We walked for over an hour and finally came to rest on a log. From here I could see the mountain top and beyond that was another, higher, mountain. Another three hours' walking would have brought us to that distant peak.

But it was already mid-morning and we decided to turn back. We ran most of the way down the forest, leaping over logs and wading through overgrown paths. Alfred led the way, moving through this terrain with grace and confidence and the knowingness of a native of the forest.

Back at the house we ate lunch and later watched a performance staged on our behalf by a cultural troupe. Men wearing
masks of forest animals – the monkey, the elephant, the fon,
the lion – danced to drumming and the tympanic rhythm of a
giant marimba played by two. The Parrots had been good hosts,
arranging things on our behalf, but never overly intrusive. I
kissed young Mungo goodbye, picking him up from the dusty
verandah, the dirt staining his pale cheeks, and wondered
whether he would one day return to Africa after he and his
parents had gone back to Britain.

With the sun in the centre of the sky, we set off for Bamenda.
The clouds had cleared and a bright crystalline daylight bathed
everything. Here and there we passed villagers dressed in their
Sunday best. A man walked across a bright ochre-coloured front
yard, his shirt a riot of colours, a child in his arms. Outside
Kumbo an elderly couple strolled together, clasping their Bibles
as they headed for the Lutheran church.

I'd noticed that Noah's driving was far slower than other
drivers and commented on this fact. I did not necessarily want
to drive, but I wanted us to travel faster. He took this as a
criticism of his driving and became sullen, comparing the Oku
road to icy mountain roads in Canada, where one had to drive
with care.

Halfway to Bamenda, we switched over. I immediately
increased the speed, rushing down the stony road, swerving to
avoid rocks, trying all the while to read the road surface. Within
minutes of driving I realised that the road had its own brakes
to speed. The rockiest stretches were always on steep slopes
or when approaching roads that linked with this main road. The
stones were signs.

Suddenly the slipperiness of the road increased and I felt less
in control of the car. I stopped. Instinct told me something was
wrong. A tyre had been ripped. The other burst tyre had been
repaired in Oku, and it was now put on the car. But we could
not risk driving the remainder of the way without a spare.
So we drove on until we came to a roadside mechanic in a
settlement.

I had been angry with Noah for implying that his experience

of driving on Canadian roads made him more qualified for driving on the Oku road than I. But he had not been entirely wrong. In my haste to be out of the countryside, I had driven too fast. More cautious driving would have preserved the tyre longer. This admission cheered Noah up.

The roadside mechanic reassured me that once he'd repaired the tyre it would wear for many miles, 'with careful driving'. As this was the second tyre we had lost, I asked the mechanic how drivers avoided destroying their tyres on the Oku road.

'If you fit tyres to the normal pressure you avoid the punctures,' he said.

'What about these rocks you have to drive over, sticking up in the road?'

'The road to Oku is a bit stony', he said; a fabulous understatement. 'You must have strong tyres,' he added.

'What about these tyres?' I said, kicking the wheel.

'Michelin tyre is good for the road but you must inflate it to the right pressure or stones will tear it.'

I asked him to test the pressure on all the tyres; did he have a gauge?

'The gauge I have here got "upset". But when I inflate the tyre I get it with the hand pressure because I'm so used to it.'

'I'll have to trust your good judgement,' I said, suppressing the scepticism in my voice, glancing at the lowering sun.

Mercifully, we reached Bamenda just before nightfall.

The restful weekend in the forest had left me feeling too energetic to pass the evening in the hotel. I had not actually seen much of Bamenda, having used it only as a resting point, and so now resolved to explore it. I began in the hotel lobby, in a shop that sold cultural artefacts. It was managed by Mamouda, a stocky, smooth-skinned young man. He was also an artist and pointed to an enormous bronze statue in the hallway – a horseman – as one of his handiworks. Smaller models were for sale.

Mamouda told me he had travelled to China, Berlin, Paris, London and the United States to participate in exhibitions. He seemed like someone who had travelled; I saw no reason to disbelieve him. A wooden carving that caught my eye – a woman carrying a fish on her head – was damaged, but he said he had a better one in his other shop, in Bamenda's main hotel. I agreed to go there with him.

Mamouda was certainly no starving artist. He drove a Japanese sports car and owned a spacious house. I went there with him, before going to the other hotel. It was sparsely furnished: a three-piece suite and an enormous Hitachi television and video unit that dominated the living-room like an icon. None of his art works was displayed.

His other shop, larger, with a greater variety of artefacts, graced the lobby of a modern hotel. The Skyline had also had ivory, but here it overflowed, in hand-sized Benin mask replicas, in smooth, highly polished eggs of a brilliantine whiteness, in mini-elephants and rhinoceroses. These animal figures, carved with great detail and sensitivity to the contours of the creatures, excited me. I had to possess one; but I remembered the ban on ivory in Britain and wondered aloud whether I should take the risk.

'Those people,' Mamouda scoffed, 'the Westerners, they interfere too much in other people's business. My people have been working with ivory for centuries. They cannot stop us. There are mountains of ivory in Cameroon alone.' He sucked his cheeks in indignation and mild anger.

'Surely,' I replied, 'it's not a bad thing that people, yes Westerners, are concerned about the fate of such a magnificent creature like the elephant. It seems to me to be a necessary movement of the age, the conservation movement. Otherwise we will kill the earth and with it perhaps ourselves as a species.'

'I agree with the wider aims of the conservationist movement,' Mamouda said. 'But sometimes these Europeans sound as though they want to keep Africa backward. We are being asked to become the nature reserve of the world, so Europeans can come and look at the animals and the trees. But we, we Africans have been living off the land and the animals for centuries. Must we stop for the Europeans' sake? You see.'

'I don't think Africans are being asked to stop exploiting the land and the wildlife it supports,' I said. 'Just to be more careful. The Europeans have destroyed many of their lands and animals. They regret it. I think there is a sense in which they want to share that lesson with Africans.'

'That's one way of looking at it,' he conceded graciously. 'But we will not stop carving with ivory.' He picked up an ivory egg and rolled it in his hand; an act that seemed both protective and sensual. I bought the mini-rhinoceros, a Benin mask and some wooden pieces. Mamouda gave me a handsome dash (a gift): some stones and a woven bag.

Mamouda said he travelled often and intended to visit Yaoundé within the next few days. We agreed to meet up there, if his trip happened.

The following morning Noah and I argued over who should drive from Bamenda. But I was uncompromising and told him that I found his driving boringly overcautious. He retorted that he had been scared throughout the drive from Douala to Bamenda, because I drove too fast and went too close when overtaking a vehicle. My defence was that he should have complained at the time, as he was a passenger and perfectly within his right to ask me to slow down. I, too, am always a nervous passenger. We agreed that I should drive halfway, which suited me as I would not be exhausted on reaching Yaoundé. I interpreted this quarrel as a sign of his full recovery and did not feel as unsettled by it as I had done by disagreements earlier in the journey.

The drive down the middle of Cameroon was uneventful. After a view of mountains, flat landscapes are always unappealing.

The dramatic beauty of Cameroon resumed in the guise of Yaoundé, the country's political capital. Bordered by deep, rich, dark greenness, it is one of the most stunning cities I have seen in Africa. The forest swaddles it, like a mother holding a child. Nowhere in the city is one far from the tranquil, profoundly mysterious feeling of the forest. Even in the city centre you sense its mighty presence, as though it were waiting with an inexhaustible patience, waiting to reclaim the land in the wake of man's mistakes. In neglected gardens and untended verges, the forest within the city flourished. But Yaoundé is no urban ruin. The city is growing. And its architecture complements the surrounding forest. Buildings expressed the spirit of Africa in their façade. I'd noticed in Bafoussam a municipal building whose exterior was designed in the shape of elongated masks. There were others in Yaoundé, a city to which the gods had been generous. For the first day in Yaoundé I remained in the hotel, which overlooked the city, and bathed my dust-filled eyes on low hills where slender cotton trees, festooned in creepers, shot upwards from grey rock, and in the distance more hills rose out of this city in the forest.

A strange thing happened to me down in Yaoundé one evening. Mamouda had driven from Bamenda and called at the hotel (no sign of Blaise). We ate a meal, then headed for town in separate cars, as he planned to return to Bamenda that night. I followed him to a crowded pavement café in central Yaoundé where a musician walked between the tables, playing a guitar, singing requested songs. In the balmy Yaoundé night, this seemed a pleasant way to pass a few hours.

When Mamouda and I parted, I discovered that my own car had been boxed in; somebody had parked directly in front of it. I blew the horn repeatedly until someone came. That person then went to find the driver of the car obstructing my exit. Minutes passed, during which my sense of annoyance mounted. The driver came and rather than move his vehicle quietly, he ranted in French. I waited until he had cleared the way; then passing him I paused to hurl my own spears of vituperations. He answered back in French and I found a Dominican phrase I'd heard the women from that island use and flung it at him. I had been expecting at least an apology from him, but instead he seemed intent on waging war. Seized by a sudden surge of anger I shouted: 'Oh, shut up you bloody French frog.' And I drove away.

Some yards down the road, I braked in the awful realisation of what I had said. In a fit of anger I had called an African a French frog, an abuse I had grown up hearing the English toss across the channel, to the French. In this nation divided between Anglophones and Francophones, through which I believed I had so far travelled with if not an objective, at least a detached eye, I had unconsciously chosen sides.

This disturbed me for many reasons, not least because as a person of African descent, I had always believed that I lacked tribal ties in Africa. Mine had been destroyed in the passage to the New World. But, of course, new allegiances had been created: I had brought to Africa my Englishness, an aspect of my identity unconsciously acquired. But no less real for that.

Cameroon was also a country trying to come to terms with its relatively new allegiances. The dilemma of its citizens is summed up in a popular Cameroonian song sung by a band called La Casque Coloniale: 'Don't throw away that pith helmet, it's mine. So it belongs to me.'

'Perhaps the chap was Francophone and abused you because you betrayed that you are Anglophone,' Eyoh suggested when I told him about the incident; how it disturbed me. He was a graduate of Birmingham University and taught Drama at Yaoundé University.

We were seated in a private club, patronised and run by Anglophones. A Senegalese academic had disapproved of my use of the terms Anglophone and Francophone. But here in Yaoundé it was used casually.

Eyoh and Bole had invited us here to taste a local dish. This club of Anglophones was crowded, and noisy with convivial laughter. But the meal, which I'd set my heart on, was long in coming.

The Anglophones, a culturally beleaguered minority, have at times felt the wrath of the Cameroonian Francophone-dominated state. They have been vociferous and obdurate opponents of the country's one-party system. The struggle for democracy here is also about the equality of the two linguistic blocs.

'We Cameroonians understand that first of all there is a battle between the Anglophones and the Francophones,' chipped in Eyoh's colleague and friend, Bole. 'Then amongst us again, we do understand that there is a battle between the *Bamblakey* and the Bassha or Burru [Cameroonian ethnic groups]. But whatever you say, when it comes to the national level, an

Anglophone, whether he comes from the Tsoubu Province or from the north will tend to identify with each other. And the Francophones will tend to identify with each other because they have common enemies.

'There was a time there were problems in this country – it was this whole identity of Anglophones and Francophones. And we were being grilled by the police. And one of the things they asked was this: "Why are you Anglophones refusing to be integrated into the nation?" I said: "But there it goes; that's the problem. If we belong to a nation and part of our history, part of our cultural history, says that one section of the country is English-speaking and the other section French-speaking, then the whole is the sum total of its parts. But by the way you are talking now it seems as if there are some parts which are at the periphery and have to be absorbed into the whole."'

Bole passionately interjected: 'There are Cameroonians who are so attached to France, that when they talk of going home it is not back to a village, it is going to Paris. We of the English tradition find this very curious. But we have our problems too. We call ourselves Anglophones, which is a misappellation, so to say, because we are Cameroonians; but because of this language divide, of English and French, we now find ourselves working hard to support a tradition which we do not quite believe in: the Anglo-Saxon tradition.'

The fish finally came. It came on a platter, a giant Atlantic sole garnished with pepper and accompanied by fried plantains and more beer. Conversation ceased and we attacked the fish with a feral ferocity, ripping its white flesh with our hands. With the fried plantains, for which I have an ardent fondness, I had not eaten a meal of such exquisite, exciting and explosive flavour in a month of travelling.

French colonial policy in West Africa was far more interventionist than that of the British. Based on the revolutionary premise of equality, it none the less assumed the superiority of Europeans, the French in particular. Africans were barbarians but they were equal and therefore they had to be converted into Frenchmen. But were the British any better?

'If you look at it in retrospect,' said Eyoh, 'perhaps the British showed a bit more respect for the cultures of the people. The intellectualism of the French led them to codify the processes of colonisation, where the English, who are a very pragmatic people, let things evolve. You don't have a British minister of co-operation, you know, bringing out television programmes which are broadcast free of charge, but the French, they have a policy of cultural survival and cultural hegemony. They do that kind of thing even at the turn of the twenty-first century.'

The cultural battle between Anglophones and Francophones is witnessed everywhere in Cameroon, in the news stands, with the English language papers jostling for space amongst the French titles, in the street signs, some in English some in French, in the television news which is read in French then summarised in English. English, however, has one advantage: it is corruptible. The French's grip over their language ensures its use in as pure a form as possible. Directions come from France. English on the other hand has been corrupted: it is the lingua franca of the common man throughout West Africa, even here in Cameroon.

These linguistic blocs, French and English, overlay a multiplicity of languages resulting from Cameroon's geographical location. It lies at one of the migratory crossroads of Africa, between north and south, between Africans of different racial stocks. Earlier, in Douala, I had seen a street-trader selling wooden and clay masks. They varied in size, some hand-sized, and design. He had told me that each mask represented a people or a tribe and were once used as a sort of passport, worn around a traveller's neck to show his tribal origin.

Cameroonian cultural activists, disturbed by the Francophone/Anglophone divide, wishing to see a more aggressive assertion of indigenous cultural identity, are thus faced with a problem. Which of the plethora of indigenous cultures should be asserted? That none is currently given expression, buried beneath the colonial legacies, is, however, a more immediate cause for concern.

The fish had been reduced to a skeleton and my tongue tingled with the sweetness of the plantain and the heat of the pepper. This was the moment for a long, cool drink of beer.

'Watch Cameroon television, for instance', said Eyoh. 'You will not believe that this is an African country, because all the people appearing on television are in suits, and in other countries when people actually do celebrate culture, they insist for instance that for a thing like the news, anybody reading the news must wear traditional clothes. What's the relationship between being Black and having your own culture that you are proud of and wearing a suit?'

The charges levelled by these Anglophone Cameroonians against their Francophone compatriots were, in the early years of independence, commonly heard across the divide between Francophone and Anglophone West Africa. It was strange to hear their echo thirty years later within the boundaries of a single nation. But it wasn't clear to me what would have satisfied my two Anglophone acquaintances, short of a separate state. A Cameroon more assertive in its Africanness, like Senegal, would still retain the tenacious French influence. Would the minority Anglophones remain resentful of the Francophones' dominance? The two academics gave me no reason to answer negatively.

Some Francophone Cameroonians I later spoke to gave a more positive impression of relations between the country's two linguistic blocs, stressing that Cameroon's dual colonial legacy had not prevented it from achieving impressive economic growth. Yet there was evidence that that growth had slowed in recent years. This leaner economic period, it seemed to me, would test a fragile unity.

*   *   *

Douala airport. The plane to Nigeria has been delayed. I am seated in a low-ceilinged room with a view over the runway. The room is crowded, and everybody is sweating. My shirt is soaked; it sticks to my chest and my back, like a second skin. The exertion required to fan myself only generates more sweat.

The most comfortable-looking person in the room is a large African lady dressed in loose-fitting native clothes. She squats on the floor, as though she were in the open air, in some compound sitting on a mat. She chews a stick while talking to her companion, who sits in the same manner, but with less composure.

Bored and irritable, I begin to write a letter to President Biya, which I would never post. It read: 'Dear President Biya, I am sitting in Douala airport in a room where the temperature rivals that of a sauna bath. Why must I suffer like this? Please install some functioning air-conditioners. But before you do that, please build a proper road to Oku, the people there deserve better.'

I leave my seat and wander to the corridor. It's marginally cooler here. A balding African stands in the middle of the hallway. He is the only person who is not sweating. I walk past him and feel the cool air. He had found a point where the air blew across the corridor.

I walk back to join him and luxuriate in the coolness.

'Welcome, brother,' he said. 'It happens every time. No plane. No air-conditioner. But if we stand here, it helps a little.'

'They should do something about it.'

'That's Africa for you,' he said nonchalantly. 'Are you Nigerian?'

'A sort of Jamaican,' I said, 'and a sort of Briton. If you see what I mean.' Frankly, at that moment, I felt this confounded country with its multiple identities had left me quite confused about my own.

TEN

TALE OF TWO CITIES

This stop, Nigeria, the first African country I ever visited, was rather like going home. I spent a month in Lagos in 1979. It was the height of the oil boom and the start of a new political direction for a country that had experienced a horrific civil war and thirteen years of military rule. I witnessed the birth of Nigeria's Second Republic on that trip. But far more engaging was Lagos, its vitality and energy, its never-ending nights; its turbulent days. I fell in love with Lagos then and knew I would always return.

I had been back many times, of course. In 1980, a year after my first visit, I took up an appointment in Ahmadu Bello University in Zaria, northern Nigeria. During the holidays – which happened more often than scheduled because strikes invariably disrupted each academic term – I would drive or fly down to Lagos, which was a day's journey by road or an hour's flight. Sometimes I drove with friends, spent a night in the nightclubs and bars and hit the road at dawn, the odours of Saturday night staining our clothes, heavy on our breaths, colouring our talk.

Arriving this time from Cameroon, I was immediately made aware that I was entering a different kind of African reality. Other arrivals had been reasonably orderly, though not without frustrations. The arrivals lobby in Murtala Mohammed airport was like a market of scarce goods, a market where shortages reigned; but everything was obtainable if one was prepared to pay the price, eschewing all ethical considerations.

The baggage rack creaked from the many jumbo-sized suit-cases and parcels. The travellers themselves wore expressions of grave concern, impatience and exasperation, and anger. Porters weaved their way between these slightly dazed figures, pushing trolleys of luggage and boxes with gusto and style.

Before I could measure the situation, I found myself being guided through immigration and customs by two Yorubas who kept on saying, 'No problem. We'll get you through.' They did and outside in the car park they sneered contemptuously at a tip of ten naira, reminding me that they would have to take care of the men at the desk. I was too grateful to argue and I gave them a hundred naira, about seven pounds.

My Lagos friends, Tunde and Elizabeth Obadina, both dis-approved. 'It's people like you who make it difficult for ordinary Nigerians. You gave them over a week's salary,' I was told reprovingly. I pleaded traveller's fatigue and was forgiven.

Despite the familiar chaos at Murtala Mohammed airport, Lagos has changed since the halcyon days of the oil boom. It has mellowed, become less brash; slowed down. But this change is relative to the late seventies and early eighties. Compared to the cities I had stopped in so far – Monrovia, Freetown, Dakar, Conakry and Yaoundé – even this calmer Lagos seemed pos-sessed of a wild urban spirit and a metropolitan grandeur that made those other places seem like villages.

There is a point on Mainland Bridge, a curve, when Lagos city suddenly comes into view: a crowded skyline of skyscrapers illumined by the powerful African sun. It is evocative of New York, but uniquely Lagos.

The original city occupies an island linked to the mainland and its neighbouring islands – Ikoyi and Victoria – by a network of expressways. These roads, built in the oil-boom years, have become sorely inadequate. At the height of the oil boom the five-mile drive from the mainland into Lagos along the Ikorodu road could take as many hours. Almost a decade of economic malaise has thinned the traffic, making the expressways more tolerable, giving one a better appreciation of the drive.

In its very structure, the city appears to lack order. Roads can suddenly disappear; houses on the same street face many different directions; grand houses sit next to buildings which look as though they have been constructed surreptitiously, unknown to the city authorities. Near the tenements favoured by modern landlords, colonial buildings – bungalows distinguishable by their verandahs, columns and zinc roofs – suffer in stoical silence.

On the jagged pavements, pedestrians in colourful agbadas (loose gowns) and safari suits and blue jeans swirl like a turbulent stream. A porter bears the shopping of an immense Yoruba woman swaddled in cloth with prints of Mercedes Benz symbols. A young lady wearing a green lace agbada daintily skips over a pool of mud. Boys and men selling newspapers, sunglasses, socks, and sundry other objects weave through the crowded, pot-holed streets. And everywhere there is music, from a record shop that also sells fans and stereos, from the ghetto-blasters of cassette sellers on bicycles, from the imam's prayer amplified in some unseen mosque.

At the motor parks below the expressway, the Danfo drivers and their mates coax passengers for districts like Ajegunle, Surulere, Mushin and Yaba. A young man in jeans and long shirt stands in the door of a moving bus, one foot in the air, now chanting, now singing, now shouting 'YabaYabaYaba. Yaba-Yaba. YabaYabaYaba.'

And in the rhythm of his voice, above the tumultuous pulse of Lagos, one can sense an order, an arrangement, a design beneath the anarchy. But the gods of this metropolis are fiendishly cryptic indeed.

Lagosians themselves either hate or love this crazy city. Those who hate it look forward to retirement in their village; Lagos life for them is a punishment or a curse inflicted by a malevolent spirit. Lagos lovers, though, will wax lyrical about the breeze that blows off the Atlantic in the afternoon; the lights trapped in the lagoons at night; drinking a cold beer on the lawns of the Federal Palace Hotel, beside the harbour. These are people who have found a rhythm in the disharmony.

Part of the city's problems derive from its origins. Known by the original inhabitants as Eko, it was christened Lagos by the Portuguese. The British who eventually colonised and created

Nigeria out of disparate peoples, built narrow streets and gave little thought to the future growth of the city. After all Nigeria, like the rest of British West Africa, was not a place to settle in.

When the oil bonanza began – in the early seventies – Lagos was suddenly flooded with the ultimate symbol of modern prosperity, the car, but no road network. The chaos that ensued was further heightened by the influx of migrants from other parts of Nigeria and the West African region. It gained the reputation of a place to make money. Country folk abandoned their hoes in places as far away as Sierra Leone and Ghana.

Naturally, in this big city, crime flourished. Lowly civil servants drove a Mercedes Benz and kept a Peugeot 504 or a Volkswagen in the garage. Politicians, soldiers and businessmen formed a triumvirate of professionals who, with the right connections, could become millionaires overnight. In this social milieu ambitions and aspirations knew no moral restrictions, except those extant in the laws which were in any case ineffectual. The law-makers and law-enforcers ranked high amongst those who were susceptible to the 'dash', the ten per cent kickback. Cynical Lagosians spoke openly of a collusion between policemen and the many armed gangs who waylaid drivers on the expressways at night, or raided parties.

The physical chaos of the city mirrored a social chaos, a season of anomie in a climate of moral uncertainty. The rules and mores, the ethical codes that had regulated men's lives and restrained their innate greed in the village or the town, melted in the Lagos heat of unlimited possibilities; the novelty of it all.

The oil-boom period and the accompanying state of moral flux in Lagos and Nigeria's history had been preceded by almost a decade of intense political uncertainty. The British political legacy – a Westminster-style system in a nation divided into three main regions – had failed to contain the ethnic passions stirred in the political arena. Two bloody coups in 1966 had been swiftly followed by a civil war which started in 1967 and ended in 1970. The Nigerian state threatened to disintegrate in a bitter fratricidal war.

The military, arguably then the only real national institution, assumed the role of arbiter, holding this fissiparous nation together. The war to keep Nigeria united against the Biafran secessionists had resulted in more roads being built between Nigerian cities. Immediately after the war, under General Yakubu 'Jack' Gowon, the nation embarked on a massive programme of unification funded by oil revenues.

But when Gowon became hesitant about the date for returning the country to civilian rule, amidst increasing corruption scandals, the lieutenant-colonels conferred and chose a new leader. Gowon was attending an OAU meeting in Addis Ababa in July 1975 when he learnt of his overthrow.

His successor, another northerner, General Murtala Mohammed, lasted only six months in office. Some Nigerians still speak of 'Murtala' as a saviour who, had he not been assassinated, would have lead Nigeria to her great destiny. Murtala's style was decisive. He popularised the expression 'with immediate effect', which is still used by older Nigerians.

Among the soldiers' many nation-building exercises was a new constitution and political system modelled after that of the United States of America. The three regions were further divided into nineteen states (now thirty); state governors were elected. And when, in October 1979, General Olusegun Obasanjo handed over power to the newly elected civilian president Shehu Shagari in a lavish ceremony befitting the most populous African state and major oil exporter, Nigerians believed a new political era had begun.

The excesses of the Shagari years mothered a new term in the Nigerian lexicon: squandermania. Billions were wasted on projects conceived with good intentions, but executed with a venality that would have shamed the robber barons of nineteenth-century America. The politicians set the pace of a manic consumerism. Nigeria produced none of the commodities – the cars, the stereos, the televisions – of modernity but these were easier to buy on the streets than the country's main export, and source of its spending power: oil.

In Zaria, Kaduna State, where I lived for two years, I once saw a sea of Mercedes Benz cars, covering five acres, at least. They seemed to appear from nowhere on property belonging

to some obscure Alhaji (the title taken by a Muslim man who
has visited Mecca). Then the government embargoed the
importation of such luxury vehicles. As the Alhaji's lake of
Mercs diminished a fabulous mosque rose in a corner of his
land. A shrine to the munificence of Allah.

Politics and access to the state's coffer's guaranteed wealth.
This induced a ruthless desperation to cling to power at any
cost. Such was the level of political thuggery and riggings in the
second election of the Second Republic in October 1983 that
one party, the Unity Party of Nigeria, refused to accept the
results. And by now the state funds had been depleted and
oil prices had fallen. Shehu Shagari's civilian government could
ignore some of its critics with impunity but not all: the military
had been stalking the civilian government with patient restraint,
waiting for the right moment. When, on the eve of 1984, the
soldiers returned, Lagosians danced in the streets. The new
regime, headed by General Muhammadu Buhari, revived memories of the Murtala years.

Citing economic mismanagement, corruption and nepotism as
its *raison d'être*, the Buhari government proceeded to declare
war against indiscipline. Errant Nigerians were whipped in the
streets; severe punishment was meted out to those too
impatient to queue in shops or bus stops. Public places were
kept clean.

When Buhari was ousted less than two years later Lagosians
danced in the streets again. The war against indiscipline had
been defeated by a groundswell of popular antipathy to the
well-meaning northern general who had dared to attempt to
clean up Nigeria, physically and morally.

I did not visit Nigeria in the Buhari years. But vestiges of his
brief rule are still discernible in Lagos. For instance, I noticed
that the everyday, mundane act of queueing is now practised
with greater ease. In the early eighties, nobody queued. Getting
on a plane, for instance, was a wild scramble; the fittest, or the
best connected with airport officials, got a seat. But trying to
board a plane for Abuja on this visit, I was roundly scolded by
an airport officer for daring to jump the queue. 'We Nigerians
don't behave like that anymore,' the fellow said with severe

indignation and a seemingly uncanny awareness that I had not been in the country for a while.

That happened at the Murtala Mohammed airport. My haste had something to do with the Nigeria I knew in the eighties; but also the fact that it was midday and I had been waiting for a plane since seven a.m. The Abuja flight had been delayed.

Abuja, conceived in the aftermath of the civil war, is one of the soldiers' ambitious nation-building projects. It is to be Nigeria's new capital. A city built in what Nigerian mathematicians calculated is the exact centre of the country, a symbol of Nigerians' determination to overcome tribalism, regionalism and religious conflict, a model metropolis devoid of the horrors of Lagos.

We reached Abuja early that afternoon. From the airport, we were driven along an empty road cut through harsh, arid savannah land. It was a flat land, but for occasional inselbergs (island rocks). The most dramatic was the Zuma rock; visible from miles away, it shoots out of the surrounding land, towering over the savannah with a powerfully mysterious presence. The indentations on the southside of the Zuma rock form the features of a face and it is the subject of many local myths.

The indigenous people of this land were forcibly moved over several years and relocated by the authorities. But some have remained; clusters of zinc-roofed mud huts, built from the red earth baked by the sun, could be seen on the road into Abuja.

The new city, which officially becomes Nigeria's new capital in October 1992, begins with a less than optimistic-looking green and white arch with the legend 'Welcome to Abuja'. The first sign of life is a small, sleepy car park, with a few taxis and buses waiting for passengers, who seemed thin on the ground. Traders sell their wares under the shade of nim and tamarind trees. Farther on, the first major buildings of Abuja begin. They are few and set off wide, treeless roads. A mosque is perhaps the most striking sight, its gold minarets sparkling in the savannah sun. But after the mosque the other buildings were distinctly unimpressive; they could have been found anywhere in the world. In this uncompleted city, there was already a ruin; the skeleton of a multi-storey building stood in solitude, looking like a creature whose flesh had been stripped by the vultures of the savannah.

It seemed incredible that so little progress had been made on a project almost fifteen years old. Nigerians blame Abuja's slow growth on the country's ubiquitous and entrenched corruption. Billions earmarked for Abuja have reportedly ended up in private Swiss bank accounts under successive administrations.

Nor are people convinced that Abuja will successfully weld the country together. Some southerners regard Abuja as a triumph of the north. 'They have built a mosque. But where is the cathedral for Christians?' a man in the car park asked me rhetorically. He came from Calabar, a city on the south-east coast with an established Christian culture.

If tribalism almost shattered Nigeria in the sixties, religious conflict threatens to have a similarly disruptive effect in more modern times. Street battles between Christian and Muslim sects have occurred in several major cities, and religious leaders have fuelled these outbreaks of violence by their increasingly belligerent utterances. That Nigeria became a member of the organisation of Islamic states has not helped to diminish this relatively new and potentially dangerous trend.

Like tribalism, however, the religious extremism that encourages violence owes something to the machinations of ambitious and unscrupulous spiritual leaders who thrive in the country's climate of anomie. Migrants to the city, overwhelmed by the size and scale of their new setting, divorced from the rituals of the countryside, often eking out a precarious living in the slums, are susceptible to the Messianic rantings of self-proclaimed redeemers.

It will require far more than a new city to contain the potential for instability inherent in Nigeria's ever-widening religious divide. All in all I left Abuju wondering how this desultory piece of urban planning could be regarded as a symbol of Nigeria's future.

*   *   *

The lateness of the plane from Lagos had meant that I, with Noah, had only been able to whisk round Abuja. Unknown to us, however, even this brief visit had aroused suspicion on the part of the security service. Back at the airport, they pounced.

The plane was again late. I killed some time in a ramshackle bookshop run by an engaging Ibo; and talked to him about the difficulties of getting books in Nigeria (though it should be said that Nigeria has a promising publishing industry). Leaving the Ibo bookseller, I went to join Noah and found him speaking to a well-dressed middle-aged Yoruba.

This man, it transpired, was a Lagos-based lawyer from Ijebu-Ode. His name was Akinsanya. We had conducted a vox-pop (random interviews with passers-by) in the Abuja car park and now decided to include Mr Akinsanya. I asked him how much he felt Abuja would contribute to greater Nigerian unity.

He felt it was too early to judge how successful Abuja would be. But he saw hope in the fact that the Abuja land did not belong to any particular tribe, unlike Lagos which is a predominantly Yoruba territory.

Mr Akinsanya felt that the threat of ethnic rivalry was exaggerated. 'No single tribe in Nigeria could threaten the unity of the country. But if two of the big tribes combined there would be danger. The civil war made Nigerians aware of their own resourcefulness. During the war the Ibos were making their own bombs. Apart from that the civil war made us aware that no single tribe can lord it over the other without the other tribe.' He believed, however, that the Ibo people still felt a great hurt because the unity of the nation had overridden their secessionist ambitions. 'But if you're going to be in the federal system you have to make some sacrifices.'

I asked Mr Akinsanya whether military rule had been beneficial to Nigeria.

However, before he could answer this question, a slim, young, brown-skinned man with blue tribal marks on either cheek appeared from nowhere. He ordered that the tape recorder be turned off and all three of us accompany him to his office. We duly obeyed.

We were taken into a tiny office, where another, older man

sat. He introduced himself and the man who had interrupted us as members of the State Security Organisation. He wanted to know who we were and why we were using a tape recorder in the airport.

Through the window, I could see the plane touch down on the tarmac.

Mr Akinsanya was quick to answer the questions. Dressed in a blue lace agbada and carrying an attaché briefcase he was clearly a man of some status. He now invoked it. 'Officers,' he said as if addressing a courtroom, 'I am a Nigerian citizen, a highly respected lawyer and regular tax payer. These gentlemen asked me to answer some questions, which I was in the process of doing when your colleague interrupted us. As far as I am concerned I have done nothing wrong, and demand the right to leave.'

The two officers conferred with their eyes and then gave Mr Akinsanya permission to leave. He departed without saying farewell.

Then the officers turned on us. Noah ran through his now much practised BBC producer's introduction, injecting a suitable humble tone designed to ensure that we were released on time to catch the Lagos plane – the last of the day – which was by now filling up.

The officers listened without interruption, then the older man said, 'You may go. But we will have to confiscate the tape recorder and tape.'

Thus began a furious round of bargaining. The tape recorder was replaceable; but the tape in the machine contained a day's work. After protestation from us, the senior officer conceded to us taking the machine, but we would have to leave the tape. The last call for the Lagos plane was announced.

Noah agreed to leave the tape. At this point I interjected and said 'No' emphatically. I pleaded and begged and when I saw they were unmoved, I played my last, desperate card: I assumed the role of Oga (a big man, an important person). In a passionate torrent I spoke of my days as a lecturer in Ahmadu Bello University, how my students were now important people in government, how they had offended me by implying that this visit, intended to gather information for a programme which would enhance outsider's understanding of this great country, was criminally motivated.

Then I feigned anger: 'How dare you threaten to confiscate my research material and undermine my quest for knowledge and truth. You will pay for this insult. I will not leave here without that tape. Take me to your boss and explain to him why you are detaining me and that your action has caused me to miss my plane, and I will not sleep in anything less than a five-star hotel which your organisation will have to pay for.'

Sweat was pouring down my face. The two conferred with their eyes again. Then the senior officer granted us permission to leave with the recorder and the tape. I shook their hands, gave them Allah's blessings; and we grabbed our belongings and dashed for the plane.

Out in the parched heat of the runway, they had just started to remove the stairs to the plane. We were allowed to board. I passed Mr Akinsanya, comfortably ensconced in a window seat, his eyes averted in shame.

Once seated I released a loud, nervous laugh, which Noah echoed. After that I slumped into a silence of emotional exhaustion that would last until the next morning.

*　　　*　　　*

A meal of bitter leaf stew afflicted me with a tender stomach on my first Lagos day. It brought back memories of why I terminated my 1979 visit. A day of constant pain had forced me to visit a clinic. There, I waited in a queue behind a man whose arm looked as though it had been ripped open by a machine. After receiving a prescription from the doctor, I resumed my place in the queue behind the young man. I saw him go behind a thin curtain, which was partly open. He was given two injections and some pills. The same treatment for my painful stomach

awaited me. The next day, the pain unabated, I booked my
flight out of Lagos.

Nevertheless, I would not allow that memory or the tenderness of my stomach to keep me inside. It was a Saturday, I
wanted to see a football game. The stadium was on Lagos
island and I found a taxi-driver to act as our guide as well. He
introduced himself to Noah as Peter, but he'd told me his name
was Olu.

We were early for the game and so decided to take a closer
look at Tafawa Balewa Square, named in honour of Nigeria's
first prime minister, killed in the country's first coup in 1966.
The gates to the square are topped by four horses, their fore-
legs raised, as though they were descending on one from the
sky. The horse as a nation's symbol is unique to Nigeria in West
Africa. And it originates properly in the north, where Islam was
spread by the horse in the jihad of the nineteenth century. The
jihad, led by the legendary Usman dan Fodio, was slowed and
eventually contained by the forests of the south.

I thought it might be a good idea to improvise something for
the tape recorder beside the gate. Before we could finish a
policeman approached. He was tall and wore a frayed khaki
uniform and his eyes were hidden beneath the peak of his
battered hat. He demanded to know what we were doing and
wanted to see our ID papers. These were duly produced but
he pressed for further papers.

The game was due to start soon and I could see that unless
we extricated ourselves from the policeman's clutches we would
miss the game. Remembering how the Liberian journalist Isaac
Bantu had dealt with a policeman I immediately changed my
tone and said: 'We are not doing anything illegal. And we are
trying to get to a football game. *Abi?*' You hear? The policeman
flinched and allowed us to leave. I had not used the expression
'*Abi*' in years. But it seemed to have a magical effect.

The Lagos stadium was only half-full, as this was a pre-season
match between Standard Bank and the Benue XI. A merciless
heat raged inside the stadium. Men fanned their faces with
newspapers and handkerchiefs and held loud conversations with
friends in distant seats. Now and again a disagreement flared

up; angry voices in aggressive tones, their meaning incomprehensible to me, exchanged abusive-sounding words. In this
Lagos stadium, the supporters of the opposing sides were not
separated. They played out the rivalry in words.

Football, the sport of the British working class, has found a
natural home in Nigeria. As in its country of origin, this game
serves to displace tribal rivalry, relocate it in a stadium and
provide potentially non-violent outlets for tribal aggression.
Watching the game and the spectators I couldn't help thinking
that a flourishing football culture in Nigeria would help to heal
Nigeria's ethnic wounds.

The game itself was unremarkable. The hard, dry, uneven
ground caused the ball to bounce awkwardly. The players could
do little more than kick and chase it, though there was the
occasional sparkle of footballing genius.

My ability to fully appreciate the game might have been dulled
by the heat. I simply could not stop sweating. It was at half-time
that I finally figured out why I was so uncomfortable. My
clothes, bought mostly in London and supplemented in Dakar,
were too thick. All the men wore loose-fitting long shirts, and
agbadas made out of cotton. When they walked, the light breeze
caused their clothes to flutter. I imagine the larger agbada
helped to trap the air, keeping its wearer cool.

This was not the first occasion on which I noticed the sartorial
elegance of Nigerians. Some nights before I'd attended a literary
award evening; had been struck by the effort that people put
into their dress, the billowing white agbadas of men and women
on the breeze-swept terraces of the Eko Hotel, the Atlantic
roaring somewhere in the darkness.

*   *   *

Dr Dora Chidzea lives in a cul-de-sac in Ikeja, a sprawling
suburb on the Lagos mainland inhabited mostly by people who
made their wealth in the seventies, the oil-boom years when

Lagos mushroomed. Her house, shaded by vast mango trees, hidden behind high walls, occupies the cul-de-sac together with a half-built house. The skeleton of some poor soul's dream, unfinished perhaps because of a lack of funds, a grey, weather-beaten monument to overambition; windowless, doorless, roofless, overrun with the vines and bushes that can so quickly mock a Lagosian's urban dreams.

Dr Chidzea works mainly from home, writing newspaper articles and managing her clinic, which is elsewhere in Ikeja. A handsome, well-built woman in her forties, she exudes authority and confidence.

She describes herself as an 'Ibo from Bendel state' and some-one whose range of activities extend from regular participation in village associations to the executive position of a UK-based international body. This made her a good person to talk to about the village and city, how much Lagosians were divided between the two.

'I doubt that village life has been lost,' she said. 'The problem is that the older you get, you find that you need the village. When you are in transit, when you are in secondary school and university and you are young and strong and ambitious and you are looking everywhere, the village seems to have lost its hold, and you don't seem to care.

'But when you are through and you finally come to settle, you have a wife, you have a husband, you start a family, you start asking the question where do you come from. The children ask where do we come from, where is our home. You find that you are not well educated in terms of knowing yourself, so you go back to your roots.

'We find that as we get to our middle ages and beyond, a lot of people who thought they had dropped the villages and the tradition start going back. Now you can see people with doctor-ate degrees, having chieftancy this and chieftancy that, because they want to belong.

'The village is holistic, because that is where they come and they say: "Who are you?" They don't say: "How much money do you have?" They don't say: "What is the university you went to?" They say: "Who are you?"'

'By that they mean: What is your genealogy, what is your root? So you say, I'm the daughter of so and so or the son and so on. And if the so and so you mention means something in the community you stop. If it doesn't, you say I am the daughter of so and so who is the son of so and so and then the daughter of so and so until you get to the place where the name means something.

'And once you have identified yourself at the level at which you are understood, then they say: "Ah, welcome my son", or "Welcome, my daughter". Then they tell you this is where you belong, this belongs to you, this is not yours and so on. So there is this cohesion, this continuity.

'And there is also this thing about the traditional rulers, you know. They are there; they are institutions like a big tree that when you grow up the tree is there and when you die the tree is still there.

'These institutions are there. They help to give stability and tradition to the community, which the central government of Nigeria can't. You know this country, we change governors and presidents all the time. So the centre has a certain kind of meaning. But in the final analysis, for the day to day survival of an individual, they know who they are because they know their roots.

'That's why I doubt that the question of tradition and the village will ever go. Nobody is going to take that land. Who? Which government? Who is the father of the child who says you should give your inherited land to who?

'He can say it in Lagos, but when he comes to the village, he has to pay respect to the traditional ruler. Then the traditional ruler will say: "Come, my son. Did you say I should give up my ancestral land?" He can't answer it. That is why the traditional rulers, the Chiefs, the Obas, have remained and I think they will remain.'

A praise-song for the village and tradition. Dr Chidzea's lyrical defence would probably find agreement with most Lagosians. One does not belong to a city; one works there to earn the funds to build a house in the village. On retirement, or sooner, the anonymity, the alienation, the unbelongingness of the city are replaced by a rural life of stability, of certainty, of antiquity.

Dr Chidzea implied that in Nigeria the wind of modernity, bringing with it Western ways, was not blowing across some barren, blank landscape.

'It will have an uphill struggle. It will try to destruct. For that is the word: destruct. To succeed in taking over? I doubt it. Because what we are witnessing here is a cultural reawakening, which is saying to people: "Embrace Western civilisation, enjoy what you can. But you are not what you have learned. You are what you are because of where you come from."'

The civil war marks a watershed in Nigerian history. It is a recurrent theme in popular fiction, and it serves to remind Nigerians of what could happen should they fail to arrive at the right formula for national unity. The defeated side, the Ibos, are now fully integrated into the nation, but not without some bitterness. I asked Dr Chidzea, an Ibo, how much importance Ibos attached to the memories of the civil war.

'I was a student in the United States during the civil war. I felt so bad. The very first book I published in my life, was published during the civil war, a book of poetry. The emotions were so hard, so painful and difficult that they had to be expressed, and they were done in rather young, violent poetry.

'But the memories have more or less started to lose their sharp edges for the people who were alive then. The youth who were born after the civil war don't really understand. So I can't really speak for all the Ibos. Those who were caught in it still feel apprehensive; they still feel that they have lost something. Although they have no evidence to show that they are any less Nigerian than the others. But they are not as bold and forthright as they used to be. The Ibo man before the civil war was said to be forthright. If he wanted something he said it. If something was one colour, he said so and he didn't care. Now he thinks a couple of times before he says it. Self-preservation has become a priority.'

Dr Chidzea runs several practices, including one at an international hotel and a specialist practice for dealing with hypertension and stress – a major killer in Lagos. Her patients aren't always convinced of the efficacy of modern medicine.

In her general practice, she often gets people coming in with malaria or fever. 'After the diagnoses you ask if the person is allergic to chloroquine or what not. He says no. You give him the treatment and tell him to come back. You don't see him again for a month. Then he returns and tells you that after the first injection he didn't feel too well. So he went to the village to see the native doctor, the *babalawo*, and he discovers that it was the uncle's wife that is putting herbs on him. So they start to kill chickens and goats to cure him. And in the process, they will be giving him herbs. This time he's back. He's picked up hepatitis, in addition.

'This is not to paint a negative picture of traditional medicine because my grandmother was a traditional doctor. In fact it's because of her that I decided to study medicine. I worked with her when I was a little girl. We went into the bush and got the herbs. So I got interested in medicine.

'There are places for herbs. For some reason educated women when they are in their middle life, they seem to lose their direction and seek herbs. It may be that they are suffering from other problems, you know this is a polygamous system, the husband may be seeking a younger wife; somewhere along the line they tend to get disoriented. Look for quick solutions in every direction. A middle-aged woman with high blood pressure knows the medicine for it, but believes that it's not high blood pressure, but due to somebody touching her, so she goes to seek herbs again and again.'

Dr Chidzea's description of her patients' behaviour reminded me of a colleague in my Ahmadu Bello University days. An American-educated social scientist whose lifestyle outwardly epitomised the new Nigerian, he was nonetheless deeply superstitious. One day I found him shaking feverishly in his office. He explained that he had that morning forgotten an amulet which he had bought from a priest to protect him against evil. Without it he felt weak and vulnerable, exposed. He had refused to see any students that morning and was waiting for a certain hour, a safe time, when he could make the five-minute drive back home to retrieve his amulet.

The two physical spaces occupied by Nigerians, the city and

the village, are also separate cultural spaces. Part of the observable turmoil in Lagos owes much to an unresolved conflict between urban and the rural worldviews. Perhaps in decades to come a more organic relationship will have evolved between the old and the new. But I could not help feeling that Dr Chidzea's patients would for many years only regard her form of medicine as a supplement to the cures used by their ancestors.

*   *   *

One of my many frustrations on this journey was not getting to northern Nigeria, to Zaria and Kaduna and Kano. Zaria and the Ahmadu Bello University campus gave me an experience which has served me for life. But time simply did not allow it. Nigeria is like that. The point of entry is where one tends to spend most time, north and south being almost like two different countries. The north is savannah territory, at its most extreme desert, the beginning of the Sahara. The south is rain forest, and swamps and deltas on the Atlantic coast. But between ocean and desert, between the majestic heights of the iroko tree of the rain forest and the regal gait of the haunting baobab trees of the savannah, are peoples who share many cultural similarities.

I was reminded of the oversimplification inherent in the north-south notion by a former ABU colleague, now Nigeria's National Director of Culture – Sule Bello. In fact, Sule Bello and I were rather more than colleagues. About the same age, we were young lecturers in the same faculty, in a small community where work and leisure happened in the same place with the same people.

But even those days Sule Bello seemed like a young man destined for something. Much as he played, he always disappeared for long enough to complete a chunk of work on his doctoral thesis. Other young lecturers, burdened by their teaching duties, and distracted by universal campus distractions, had no time for those lengthy dissertations.

His office is in the grounds of the National Theatre, a vast tiara-shaped structure – designed by Hungarians – and one of the landmarks of Lagos.

Sule pointed out that there are many important socio-cultural similarities between communities in the north and south. For instance, there were shared established kingdoms, from the Sokoto Caliphate to the Ilorin Emirate (in the middle of Nigeria, Kwara state) and the *alafin* of Oyo. These were all centralised states, sharing similar institutions and mores and values. Then there were the segmented states like Borno in the north, among the Tivs in Benue in the middle belt and among the Ibos in the south.

'These segmented communities, their social structures, the values, their belief systems, ancestor worship – they are all similar.'

Sule believes that these ancient similarities have been supplemented by more modern ones, as a result of increased contact between Nigerian peoples. A distinctly Nigerian identity is in formation, nullifying ethnic rivalry.

Nevertheless, he shared my concern about the potentially destabilising effects of a growing rift between Muslims and Christians. That Nigeria joined the Organisation of Islamic States has enraged some Christian leaders, some of whom have spoken in apocalyptic terms of a showdown between followers of the two religions. We agreed that whether the tension between the two religions erupted into conflict would depend very much on the conduct of religious leaders.

'All the debates we have had on the OIC have not affected the majority of Nigerian people. I believe there are forces working towards a conflict, but it's not relevant to the majority of the people. At the moment it's largely a conflict between certain élites who have an interest in keeping it alive. In Nigeria, you find that, especially in the western parts, people, communities, houses, families are divided into different religions. It's not uncommon to find in some houses Christians, Muslims and even ancestor worshippers. There is an environment of religious tolerance at the lower levels.'

Sule's reference to the religious plurality found in western

Nigeria – Yorubaland – was important. The Yorubas seem to have an amazing capacity for worshipping in many different temples. Most of the southern Muslims are concentrated amongst them, though far outnumbered by Christians. But the prevalence of these two major religions has not resulted in the disappearance of the Yorubas' traditional religion. Ife, historically the spiritual centre of Yorubaland, retains that function.

In northern Nigeria, where Islam predominates, however, it is difficult to recognise what is uniquely Hausa or Fulani (the largest ethnic groups there). Are there aspects of northern culture which are unique to the region, separate from Islam?

'In the northern parts, Islam, because it has been there for centuries, has become indigenised. Take the mosque: in the early days the sculptural design of the mosque was specific to this part of the world. In terms of calligraphy, northern Nigeria has its own style which is not found in other parts of the Islamic world. This is what I mean by indigenised. But there are still pockets of non-Islamic worship, ancestor worship, in the north.'

We then talked for a while about the heady days of civil rule, when we were both lecturing in ABU. I was pleased to hear Sule discuss politics without resort to the clichés of Marxism, which was then in vogue among many lecturers, stifling the intellectual creativity, the new ways of seeing, that this young nation needs. But our recollection of the Second Republic was occurring at the moment when the country was poised to return to civil rule. The soldiers who seized power in 1985 have set 1992 as the year for the full resumption of democracy. I asked Sule whether he felt optimistic about the birth of the Third Republic. Here I was rather hoping that he would give me a critical answer. But it was an unrealistic wish. He was now, after all, a highly placed state functionary.

'There are various things which the government has introduced, which are designed to assist in the development and promotion of a democratic culture. There is an institution of democratic studies; the mobilisation of rural folk. As well the establishment of parties which are not controlled by any individuals.

'These, I think, are positive factors in the evolution of the

Nigerian political system. There could be some impediments from those people a little bit aggrieved because they have been banned from politics. Their political future looks bleak in the scheme of things. But in the final analysis, whether democracy succeeds will be determined by our willingness to implement the new system. No matter how well designed a political system, if people are not committed to it, it will not work. But it is clear that the government wants to restore democracy.

'We made two important mistakes in the past. The various political parties could not arrive at some kind of compromise. You can have conflict but this conflict has to be resolved in an agreed way.

'And there was a tendency for people to insist that their part of the country should be maintained, have certain privileges denied to others. That was a mistake. They have now seen that in guaranteeing for others you guarantee for yourself.'

It is Sule Bello's generation which will lead Nigeria into the twenty-first century. Young men and women who grew up in the shadow of the civil war and came to maturity in a climate of regret for the divisiveness that almost tore the country asunder. Knowing that generation as I do, I am confident that ethnicity will never again have the disruptive impact that marked the first decade of independence. However, the path to stability and prosperity, which Nigerians believe to be their destiny, is haunted by many demons, the shapes of which are not always predictable. A key factor in that future, though, will be the military: will they remain in the barracks regardless of how chaotic civil rule might appear? Will they give political parties, the judiciary, voters and public opinion the opportunity to determine the country's course?

Abuja is a symbol of Nigeria's hopes for the future and if it succeeds the soldiers who initiated it will be long remembered.

Meantime sweaty, overcrowded, manic-paced Lagos remains Nigeria's premier city. A status which it is unlikely to lose, even after its official relegation.

ELEVEN

'ROOTS'

I had an unusual experience in Lagos one night. I had passed most of the night in an Ikoyi nightspot – Jazz '90. I arrived back at the hotel about an hour before dawn. Standing at the hotel entrance, I was approached by a slim young lady with the unmistakeable look of fear on her face; a familiar face, reminding me of somebody I knew in England.

She first addressed me in Yoruba and immediately switched to English. 'I'm in trouble. I need your help,' she said. She glanced behind her, to a crowd of people who milled about at the door of the hotel's casino.

'What kind of help?' I asked.

'Please walk with me. Around the car park. Please.'

I had heard too many horrific stories of robbery and murder in Lagos to respond with immediate chivalry, however genuinely distressed she sounded. But after a moment's thought, I could see no possible harm in agreeing to her request: the hotel was fronted by a circular driveway, with armed security men at the street entrance; a few sleepy porters sat yards from us.

So we stepped on to the driveway and began walking in the direction of the casino.

'You're not Yoruba,' she said.

'No. I am a Jamaican.'

'But you look so much like us.'

She walked close beside me, her shoulder brushing my arm.

'What kind of trouble are you in?' I asked. We were passing

the casino now. Muffled voices rode on the breeze, with the smell of tobacco and alcohol. Either she didn't hear me, or she chose not to answer. We walked on in silence.

Some yards on I sensed that we were being followed. I turned round and saw two men, a stocky African and a young blonde European.

'Sola,' the African shouted.

'Please, let's carry on. Ignore them,' she said.

'Is that your boyfriend?' the white man called out. He was clearly drunk.

I felt the tension in her body as she moved even closer to me.

'I'll get you, Sola,' the white man called out again. 'You'll be mine. I'll get you.' Desire and threat echoed in his slurred speech, which the breeze from the Atlantic whipped past my ears.

The footsteps of the two men receded as we neared our starting point.

'Will you be OK now?' I asked. I need not have put this question to her, because the two men were not far away; they were outside the casino watching us.

She gripped my arm and stared at me with frightened childlike eyes. She said: 'Please, I have a friend. He's one of the taxi-drivers. He looks after me. But he won't be back for a while. Can you wait with me? Please.'

I had been up all night and now, with the faint glow of dawn on the horizon, desperately wanted to sleep. But she was obviously in some sort of trouble. My conscience would not allow me to abandon her. I told her I had to rest, but she could wait in my room.

She left a message with one of the sleepy porters and followed me up to my room. Here, under the brighter light, I saw her properly, saw how a man could hunger for her. She had the unblemished darkness of polished ebony and beneath her high cheekbones were fulsome lips that looked as though they had been carved. A trace of ruby red lipstick clung to those lips. She was slim, almost skinny; her loose-fitting linen dress, far from concealing, accentuated her bony hips.

I offered her some water, which she accepted, and opened the door to the balcony. A salty breeze billowed the curtains and stirred a vague scent of jasmine and sweat. She slumped into the armchair and gulped the water. I stood by the balcony door, sipping my own water, looking out at the lagoon and the ocean, fighting off the sense of fantasy which had settled on me since meeting her.

'You didn't answer my question,' I said.

'What question?' The water seemed to have revived her. I detected a note of aggression in her voice.

'What kind of trouble are you in?'

'Does it matter?'

'If I saved somebody from drowning, I would be curious how he fell into the water, whether, maybe, he did it deliberately.'

'Sorry,' she said in what was almost a whisper. 'That White man has been troubling my life for weeks. Every night he is waiting for me.'

'You owe him something?'

'No,' she said firmly, suddenly sitting upright. 'I went with him one night. He was violent. Very violent. I did not want to go with him again. But every night he is looking for me with that Bendel boy.'

'The African with him?'

'Yes. I thought you were a Yoruba. You look so much like a Yoruba. That's why I came to you for help.' Her voice trailed off into a whisper again.

Silence. With heavy eyes, I gazed at the vast sky of swirling grey clouds that hung over the sea. A sea which in the distance and from the tenth floor of the Eko Hotel seemed unmoving. But the pounding waves on the beach revealed otherwise.

The phone rang, causing Sola to stand up. It was the call she had been expecting; her taxi-driver friend had returned. She reacted coolly to the news. She adjusted her dress and perfunctorily brushed her hand through her permed hair.

'Thank you very much,' she said at the door.

'That's all right,' I said with more nonchalance than I intended to convey. '*Odabo*.'

'You are a Yoruba!' she exclaimed.

'Maybe I was, a long time ago,' I said as simultaneously a powerful surge of exhaustion rocked my body.

I closed the door and went out on to the balcony. Dawn had

fully arrived now. A heavy mist hung over the sea. In the nearby lagoon, the first fishermen, two matchstick-like figures, slowly glided across the water in a canoe. The one standing hurled and hauled a net that sparkled in the early morning light.

As I stood there on the balcony, I felt a terrible emptiness, as though I had lost something precious, vital, irreplaceable. The girl's words echoed in my exhausted mind: 'I thought you were a Yoruba. You look so much like a Yoruba.'

Not for the first time I wondered which of the African tribes I originated from. Who were my gods? What were my myths? What were my rituals of celebration for new life, for death? By what symbols did I make sense of the universe? What was my language? What was my name?

These were familiar questions, yet they came to me with a curiously sharp, unfocused pain, as if something had erupted in my body or mind.

It was a discomforting end to what had been an enjoyable night of music and laughter. I thought about it for many days afterwards, without arriving at any firm conclusions. Before that Lagos morning, I regarded Africans or Europeans who were aggressively assertive in their tribalism or nationalism with the quiet disdain of a person who, lacking such emotional ties, believed himself to be a superior being, tomorrow's man. But that morning made me aware that I have in the past hungered for an identity more concrete than 'world citizen', that I wear a mask which sometimes slips. Perhaps if I had arrived at this rootlessness, this lack of belonging, by a less violent route than the middle passage, the slave plantations of the Caribbean and migration as a child, I would never hunger for roots, which I know, in my composed moments, are irrevocably lost.

I no longer felt superior to the person with strong tribal ties. It intrigued me, though, that it was a Yoruba who, mistaking me for one of her own people, caused this revision. Because the Yorubas are arguably Nigeria's most tribally minded people.

Of the West Africans brought to the New World, their culture has shown extraordinary resilience. Worshippers of Shango – the Yoruba god of lightning and justice – are found throughout the Americas. So too is Ogun, the god of iron and war. In parts of Brazil, the gods of the Yoruba religion are twinned with Catholic saints to create a syncretic religion, outwardly Christian but profoundly African.

And, despite the strength of Islam and Christianity amongst Yorubas within Yorubaland, their own superstition – as opposed to the superstitions of others – is still widely believed in. Every Yoruba adult knows where to find a babalawo, a medicine man, possessor of ancient and arcane herbal arts.

An older colleague of mine in my ABU days, an American-trained social scientist, once confessed to me that without the protective charm prescribed for him by a babalawo he suffered acute anxiety. He feared for his life. He came from Ilesha in Yorubaland and was a devotee of Ogun.

The Yoruba pantheon of gods consists of four hundred and one Orisas (gods), with Olodumare as the supreme being, 'the creator of heaven and earth and all beings and things'. There are no cults or temples of Olodumare; he is worshipped through prayer and invocation. Rather the Yorubas build shrines and temples and create cults around specific divinities, who are regarded as Olodumare's intermediaries and functionaries.

Ogun is the most vital of these divinities. According to Yoruba mythology, when the divinities were first coming to inhabit the earth they came to a thicket and could not cut their way through it. Each of the divinities tried but failed until Ogun volunteered his services and cut the path through with his sharp machete. As a consequence all the divinities hailed him as great. He is called Osinmale – chief among the divinities.

In a famous Yoruba legend with many variations – all of which focus on civil war, rebellion and other forms of political conflict – the warrior Ogun sentences himself to eternal isolation after unwittingly slaying some villagers in a frenzy of rage brought on by their refusal to serve him palm wine.

He is believed to be the divinity of iron and war and pre-eminently the tutelary divinity of hunters, blacksmiths, gold-smiths, barbers, butchers, and in modern times the mechanics, the lorry- and taxi-drivers – indeed all workers in iron and steel. No Yoruba hunter goes on a hunting expedition without paying respect to Ogun; no soldier goes to war without offering appropriate sacrifice to the divinity; no lorry-driver considers himself safe until offering is made to Ogun. Indeed, one explanation proffered for Nigeria's epidemic of accidents is that the professional road-users – lorry- and taxi-drivers – believe themselves immune from death as long as they offer sacrifices to Ogun. A taxi I saw on the Ikorodu road bore the legend: 'Blessed by God, guided by Ogun.'

Many contradictory qualities and images are associated with Ogun. He is a terrible figure dressed in red, a violent warrior, fully-armed and laden with potent charms and medicines to kill his foes. He is also society's ideal male, a leader known for his sexual prowess who nurtures, protects and relentlessly pursues truth, equity and justice.

Wole Soyinka, a Yoruba, a Nigerian and Africa's only Nobel Prize winner for Literature, readily acknowledges his debt to the great body of Yoruba mythology; and constantly reminds quarrelsome followers of Islam and Christianity that they are 'both slaves of completely alien religions anyway. And the traditional religions, the authentic religions have one lesson . . . religion is a purely internal thing, it is a spiritual thing, it is a ceremonial, ritualistic thing. And it's also a bottomless fount of metaphors for one's creative existence.'

With that kind of attitude it's understandable how a younger Soyinka could have pronounced with derision on Negritude: 'A tiger doesn't have to assert its tigritude; it pounces.'

I met Mr Soyinka briefly in his Abeokuta office, an hour's drive from Lagos. We talked mainly about Nigerian literature, but it was he who reminded me that there is in Jamaica a village called Kuta – a corruption of Abeokuta – by its inhabitants, the older members of which call themselves Anago people (a Dahomean term for Yorubas).

So maybe the distressed girl outside the Eko Hotel at the end of that weary night was right after all. If, for whatever reason, my need for tribal roots – displaced, among most African descendants as a need for racial roots – should ever become irresistibly overpowering I might find satisfaction amongst the Yorubas. Or amongst a people from whom the majority of Jamaicans are descended, Ghanaians. Ghana was the next stop.

TWELVE

A CULTURE OF SILENCE

After the speed and fury of Lagos, Accra, the Ghanaian capital, brought to mind a large suburb. The traffic on its many tree-lined streets moved at a crawling pace; people strolled on the roadsides; there were no cautionary tales of desperate gunmen lurking in the shadows, at least not for ordinary citizens.

In contrast to this rather sedate pace of life, the Atlantic Ocean here is vigorously restless. But this does not prevent Accra citizens from flocking to the sea on Sundays. I spent my first full day, a Sunday, recovering from Lagos on an Accra beach. It was a desolate stretch of golden sand when I got there, but as the giant waves of the morning receded beneath a fierce afternoon sun, a vast swarm of people gathered. I watched whole families strip and immerse themselves in the warm ocean, as if enacting an ancient ritual. Surrounded by these Ghanaians at play, I forgot I was in a country which Ghanaian exiles in London had described to me as repressive and run by a sinister state machinery.

Next day, I returned to where I had begun. I had started my journey in Liberia, a nation originally created for African-Americans who dreamt of freedom *in* Africa. I was now in a country which had earlier this century symbolised African-American dreams of freedom *for* Africa.

Ghana was the first African nation to gain independence. This was achieved in 1957 under the leadership of Kwame Nkrumah, who had studied in the United States and lived in London before returning to lead the nationalist struggle here. Like Senegal's Léopold Senghor, Nkrumah's contact with detribalised, racially conscious Africans from the diaspora had a profound influence on how he viewed Africa and Africans. Senghor's encounter with those foreign Africans contributed to his becoming the champion of Negritude while Nkrumah became the champion of its political equivalent: pan-Africanism.

Ghana's independence wasn't just for Ghanaians, it was for Africans everywhere, the continent, and the Americas. Nkrumah named his country's shipping line after Marcus Garvey's Black Star Line – the company started by Garvey to ship African descendants in the West back to Africa. And he called on 'the sons and daughters of Africa domiciled in the West' to return to Africa.

Among those who responded positively were Nkrumah's comrades in his years of exile: the Trinidadian-born George Padmore, C.L.R. James, another Trinidadian, and the American W.E.B. Du Bois.

C.L.R. James only visited Ghana, but he sustained a critical dialogue from a distance with Nkrumah for many years. C.L.R. recognised in Nkrumah a man who 'was the inheritor of the centuries of material struggle and intellectual thought which the Negro people in the United States had developed from all sources in order to help them in their effort to emancipate themselves'.

Du Bois was a scholar and political activist best known as one of the founders of the National Association for the Advancement of Coloured People and for his brilliant essay, 'The Soul of Black Folks'. He also gained some notoriety for his uncompromising opposition to Marcus Garvey's 'back to Africa' movement. In a scathing article written in 1923 – when the Garvey movement had begun to decline – Du Bois argued that 'American-Negroes' were better off without Garveyism because it urged them to: '"Give up! Surrender! The Struggle is useless; back to Africa and fight the white world."'

Yet W. E. B. Du Bois died in Africa, here in Ghana. His last years were spent working on an *Encyclopedia Africana* – at the behest of Kwame Nkrumah – in a pleasant colonial-style residence, which today houses a memorial to him.

I went there to pay my respects, and to speak to Efua Sutherland-Addy, director of the W. E. B. Memorial and Institute. A large brown-skinned woman with a rather grave face and a mercurial smile, she readily acknowledged the enormous contradiction in Du Bois' life.

'But Du Bois was lucky to have lived long enough to be able to evolve,' she said. 'By the time you get to 1945 and the pan-African Congress in Manchester he gets very interested in ensuring that Africa must indeed be liberated as part of this whole pan-African experience. But he didn't necessarily let go of the idea that people of African descent on the American continent should stay there and benefit from what they had done.

'He began to see the possibility of the realisation of a dream; the fact that the liberation of the African continent had a great deal to do with his own liberation and the liberation of the people in the diaspora. Therefore it became almost a natural cause to fight for, to make sure that all people of African descent wherever they lived were liberated.'

I asked Efua Sutherland-Addy how those who had answered Nkrumah's call had fared in Ghana and whether Africans in the diaspora were still drifting back to Africa.

'Those who came in to Ghana in the wake of independence, were professionals with skills. In the late sixties we had people coming in looking for their roots, for inspiration. Up until even the late seventies they were coming in; to experience the middle-passage; an emotional experience, people going to look for their name, their family and so on. But between the mid-seventies and mid-eighties, there was some disillusionment with African self-government. There was a lack of faith in what we had become. This was reflected in a slower pace of people returning. What we have now is a revived interest. There's now even people looking for opportunities for financial investment. So the trend continues; but it's not in the same form as before and there is a good chance that it will build up again by the end of the century.'

I agreed with her forecast that there could be a revival of interest in returning to Africa. The urge for Africa will probably never again create a nation or inspire a mass exodus. In the past that urge has been strongest amongst the poor of the Caribbean and the United States. But today, forging links with Africa in those places has acquired respectability in mainstream outlets. In the United States, for example, African-American celebrities and politicians have been at the forefront of the opposition to investments in South Africa. But something even more significant has happened: peoples of African descent in the United States, known over the centuries by a variety of names bestowed on them by others, have chosen a collective nomenclature which points unambiguously to their African roots. This name-change owes a great deal to the increased prosperity and confidence of African-Americans. Efua Sutherland-Addy, who had not long returned from a visit to the States, wasn't surprised that Africa continued to exert such a hold over its descendants in the West.

'There is this feeling of a loss of identity, sort of being thrown in the soup-pan, and getting lost in there. Whereas many other ethnic groups keep their identity and they do it with a great deal of ferocity. The loss of identity caused by the slave trade and slavery will continue to bother and agitate the minds of African-Americans.'

I asked whether there were any formal procedures for accommodating African descendants who wished to return.

She smiled wryly and said: 'In Ghana we have had a very turbulent independence. The Nkrumah period was eclipsed and everything that was associated with Nkrumah, good or bad, was eclipsed. But there is something of a revival of interest in Nkrumah's vision.'

Twenty-four years after his overthrow by the military in 1966 and eighteen years after his death in exile in Sékou Touré's Guinea, Kwame Nkrumah remains a domineering presence in the Ghanaian national psyche. The city of Accra is littered with monuments built during the intoxicating years of Nkrumah's rule: a Romanesque independence arch; an obelisk in the centre of Liberation Circle; Olympic-size swimming-pools, but with diving boards caked in dust above cracked, empty pools. Quotes from Nkrumah's books and speeches are displayed in public places, newspapers regularly carry articles exploring his legacy. One night I watched a lively television debate between scholars and soldiers on the subject of Nkrumah's achievements and failures. He is to Ghana what Lenin was to the Soviet Union, Mao Tse-tung to China, Robespierre to the French Revolution.

The current Ghanaian government – the result of a military coup against an elected government – in its early years, those uncertain times when the legitimisation engineers have to work hardest, often invoked Nkrumah's name to win popular support. From Christianborg Castle, a former slave fort, the Provisional National Defence Council issues proclamations and decrees in the name of the 'revolution' which its ideologues claim to have been inspired by Nkrumah's memory.

One day the government-owned *People's Daily Graphic* carries this quote from Kwame Nkrumah: 'In this struggle we shall not reject the assistance of our friends, but we will yield to no enemy however strong.' A few days later the Chairman of the PNDC, Flight-Lieutenant Jerry Rawlings, occupies the same prominent space, though with rather less succinctness: 'A good education must necessarily have relevance to the circumstances of the environment and society and must also have a practical orientation towards the solution of the problems and development of the society.'

The PNDC's claim to be the torch-bearers of Nkrumahism is not without some truth. It has made 'the people' the focus of its policies, accelerating the growth of schools, and rural schemes. It has also created a range of structures for encouraging popular participation in local decision-making.

Learning of such progressive policies, and after my day at the beach, it puzzled me why Ghanaians in London had been so critical of their government. Some of the reasons gradually became apparent. I began to discover amongst Ghanaians a reluctance to talk politics, even taxi-drivers were reticent on this subject. I started noticing the astonishing aridity of newspaper contents. One front-page leading article opens: 'The leader of the Revolution Chairman Jerry Rawlings . . .' Its tone amounted to verbal genuflection, a far cry from the robust reportage of the Nigerian newspapers I had read days before. These Ghanaian papers carried no debates, no critical opinions on the issues of the day. After the well-stocked shelves of Dakar, Douala and Yaoundé's bookshops, the empty, dusty shelves in Accra's bookstores left me wondering how a nation like this could have given Africa a heroic figure like Kwame Nkrumah, a one-time journalist and author of several books.

Adu Boahen, a retired historian – a small, neat man with an air of pedagogical severity – describes the absence of debate in Ghana as a 'culture of silence', which is part of Kwame Nkrumah's ambiguous legacy to Ghana.

'Kwame Nkrumah, as a Black man, is probably the greatest African who has lived this century. He brought a great deal of pride and hope to the Black race. He became a symbol of Black nationalism. He also contributed enormously to the liberation of Africa.

'But as a Ghanaian, he was a disaster. He sacrificed Ghana on the altar of pan-Africanism. He left this country on the verge of bankruptcy; completely politically disunited; without any traces of democracy. He converted Ghana into a one-party state.'

From my early days of political consciousness, of my consciousness as a person of African ancestry, Kwame Nkrumah was a heroic figure, a man who stood up there in the pantheon of African heroes with Marcus Garvey, Martin Luther King, Malcolm X, Nana (a Jamaican maroon leader) and others. And it was not only me. And I was not alone: Nkrumah's portrait is commonly seen on murals in British Caribbean community centres. I'd last seen it on T-shirts in a Harlem shop window. Though I had long ceased to shower uncritical adulation on any hero, Boahen's frank appraisal of Nkrumah was none the less mildly disquieting.

Nkrumah's domestic policies did indeed have disastrous effects on Ghana. Impatient with the parliamentary process, he rewrote the constitution, arrogating to himself the power to nullify judicial decisions. He outlawed all opposition and jailed recalcitrant opponents. These anti-democratic measures were justified on the grounds of 'jet-propelled development'. Obsessed with the vision of a united, modern Africa, he seemed to have regarded the Ghanaian state as a machete to cut a path of modernity through the dense undergrowth of economic backwardness.

Boahen believes, however, that Nkrumah's emphasis on pan-Africanism wasn't entirely misplaced.

'He was probably preaching the right thing at the wrong time. In the late fifties and early sixties, at a time when most African countries had just emerged from colonialism and were thinking of how to organise independent states, how to cope with the stupendous economic problems bequeathed by colonialism, the problems of ethnicity and tribalism and so on, I don't think they were really ready to think of African unity. Now conditions are making it obvious, even to the most reactionary of African leaders, that there are so many problems which cannot be tackled on an individual basis.'

'What, then, are the obstacles to that unity?'

'In those days it was the jealousy of the newly independent African states. Each one wanted to be a boss in his own country. Now that problem is not so important. The main problem now is external forces: though we have been independent for decades, many of these independent African countries are still being manipulated by their former colonial masters. The Francophone African countries are just not independent enough. They are still considerably dominated and dictated to by the French.

'Then there is the problem of political instability. Since nineteen sixty-six Ghana has had about nine or ten different governments. How can any country ensure continuity, stability, political leadership, let alone look beyond its frontiers to transform West African unity? Nkrumah became so important because he was able to rule from 1951 to 1966. Fifteen solid years. And he had, of course, the ideas.'

Africa, it seemed to me, was in a catch-22 situation. Greater unity could only be achieved by political stability, yet that stability was a precondition for greater unity. What of the great self-appointed redeemers of African politics, the military? Had they made any contribution to solving this conundrum? Adu Boahen believed not.

'They compound the problems; they don't solve them. The citizenry should be allowed to pass judgement on properly elected governments. And if anybody, including the army, feel that the constitution is being trampled upon or being abused; then they can intervene. But not to overthrow the constitution; but rather to see that the clauses of the constitution are enforced. But what do we see? The military step in. If your excuse is that in the country, there was no freedom of the Press, no freedom of the individual and so on, come and see that the constitution is properly adhered to. But you don't come and tear up the constitution. So I don't think the military have helped.'

The only virtue Adu Boahen saw in the current Ghanaian government was that its administration involved more professional civilians than previous military regimes in the country's history.

I had come to Ghana hoping to interview Chairman Jerry Rawlings or a senior member of government, in part because I empathised with the sense of frustration which must have brought the PNDC into power. Many of the PNDC leaders are in their forties; they would have been schooled in the independence years, matured under the shadow of corruption, nepotism and inefficiency; felt deeply the disappointment of independence. When Jerry Rawlings burst on to the Ghanaian political stage, he was seen as part of what seemed – within Ghana and outside, to people like myself frustrated by Africa's stumbling – like a new, younger generation of African leaders who would right the wrongs of the recent past. This promising moment included Thomas Sankara of Burkina Faso and Liberia's Master-Sergeant Kanyon Doe. In the early eighties, pictures of Sankara and Rawlings regularly featured in London-based African publications. There was talk of a political union between the two countries. One journalist dubbed them the 'reggae generation' of African politics, because they seized power at a time when that music was at its most popular.

Sankara was later killed in a coup led by his second-incommand, Blaise Compaore. And Doe was now fighting off an invasion.

Rawlings, however, has proved himself a consummate coup survivor. He first seized power in a bloody coup in 1979, which included public executions, handed over to a civilian government six months later, then led another coup two years on. Asked when he would return power to civilians this time, Rawlings replied: 'Who is there to hand over to?' His has been the longest running political show since Nkrumah.

What exactly had they borrowed from Nkrumah? How had political power changed these young idealists? How did their form of government differ from that of preceding, and surrounding governments? Could they envisage when and under what circumstances they would return power to civilians? These were some of the questions I wanted answered.

But the Castle, as it is popularly known, is infamously difficult to enter. Letters had long been sent from London. My first attempt to see someone in authority beyond the press officer failed. Kept waiting for three hours, I stormed into the press officer's office and demanded some attention. But he politely asked me to leave until he had sorted something out. I was not especially wounded by this experience. He was scrupulously polite, unaggressive, cool almost, which took the sting out of my assault. His tone suggested, 'Brother, you can't hurry the revolution'. I knew then I would not be granted the interview I wanted, at least not within the time I had scheduled for Ghana.

So I was left to form my own impression of the PNDC government. Jerry Rawlings and his comrades undoubtedly came to power with sincere ambitions to fundamentally improve Ghana, they probably equally saw themselves as the bearers of a relit torch of Nkrumahism. Nkrumah's children, as it were. But they have merely borrowed Nkrumah's revolutionary rhetoric, denuded of pan-Africanism, while implementing his repressive policies more efficiently and to deadlier effect. Nkrumah jailed his opponents. Political dissidents in Ghana have disappeared. Each attempted coup, real or imaginary, has been followed by killings, and an increase in the number of Ghanaian exiles. Between 1982 – Rawlings's second coming – and 1986,

Rawlings vied with Liberia's Doe for the number of coup attempts purportedly quashed.

From the streets, Ghanaians have watched the lean, handsome Flight-Lieutenant Jerry Rawlings become the bloated PNDC Chairman – not unlike his Liberian counterpart, Samuel Doe. Those who feel they know his inner thoughts believe he is too afraid to relinquish power because he fears he would be hunted down by his successors. So he builds an ever more extensive, elaborate and sophisticated security network.

The Paramouncy of security taints even ostensibly positive projects. The District Councils, for instance, for which elections were held two years ago. One third of all District Council members are government appointees. Consequently the Councils are viewed with suspicion; not a place where an elected official will freely air his views. Most likely he will fear being reported by some of his fellow members as a troublemaker, a security risk.

Sadly, Ghana, for all Nkrumah's dreams and hopes, is just another poor African country ruled by an insecure, unelected government of yesterday's critics who have become today's censors: yesterday's liberators, today's jailers. And in the city, Accra, a fear-filled silence reigns.

However, I was reluctant to regard the PNDC government as just prisoners of Nkrumah's legacy. It shared too many political features with Liberia, Sierra Leone, Guinea and Cameroon for me to arrive at such a narrow conclusion. Rather, I believe there are within African countries powerful dictatorial forces rooted in traditional politics and the colonial past. The colonial powers certainly didn't rule by consent. The extremely limited 'democracy' which existed in traditional society was ineffectual in the larger and newer political units, embracing different peoples and cultures. Independence marked only the beginning of a transition from colonial and ancient ways of ruling, from disparate ethnic groups to nationhood. In the ensuing turbulence colonial and ancient forms of governance combined to dictate, to coerce, to impose order. The president, the general, the lieutenant or the sergeant becomes the modern chief – the personification of a marriage between recent and distant histories which could not be easily buried. The PNDC – and other similar West African governments – perpetuate the imprisonment of their nations in those histories because, as Guinea's Portus Diallou suggested, it is far easier to rule through decrees and proclamations. Hence one-party and military rule thrive.

Yet denying the populace a critical voice, stifling opposition in the interests of unity or order or development robs a nation of the dialogue between the rulers and the ruled which is vital for progress. Such means impede or prevent the achievement of the ends. Inefficency, nepotism and corruption flourish in the imposed silence.

It could be said, though, that Westerners make too much of the corruption of African states. One Ghanaian social scientist, Kwame Ahin, suggests that the continent's high level of corruption should be seen as a phase of primitive accumulation similar to that which happened in Europe before the industrial revolution: 'But we are not like Europe. We can't be piratical. We can't start the slave trade. The shame, of course, with our own primitive accumulation, is that so much of the stolen funds is taken elsewhere, deposited in Swiss bank accounts.'

Ahin's remark points to the danger of trying to judge Africa with Western yardsticks. After all, Western democracies are the imperfect realisation of an ideal which has been pursued for centuries and most of the economies on which such political systems are based were built on the subjugation and exploitation of regions like West Africa. West African states can hardly be expected to have reached Western levels of democracies within thirty years.

Nor has Africa's relation to the West changed with independence. Africans may now own their economies but they exercise little effective control over them. They are sellers in a buyer's market, and buyers in a seller's market. Furthermore, foreign powers have helped to create fertile conditions for dictators, one-party rule and military rule. The cold war between the superpowers carved Africa up into spheres of influence where the worth of an African government wasn't measured by how well it served its people, but by the strength of its loyalty, to the West or the East; or in Francophone West Africa's case, the French. The demise of the cold war could help to accelerate the growth of democracy on the continent. But democracy is a costly business.

It is difficult to see how Africa can benefit from this post-cold-war world, unless world trade is also governed by a new morality which recognises and eliminates the iniquitously unfair current terms of trade between poor and rich nations. Would Westerners willingly make the necessary sacrifices? I think not. More likely the continent will remain the recipient of charitable donations and aid, which are not unimportant, because they do relieve human suffering, but which cannot correct the underlying inequality between nations.

This is one reason why Nkrumah's pan-African dream remains so crucial to the continent's future: the economic arguments in its favour are incontestable. But Nkrumah's haste – possibly, too, the influence of African descendants in the West – blinded him to the innumerable cultural and political divisions in Africa which cannot be overcome by the appealing logic of economics alone. There are, however, strong political arguments in favour of unity. West Africa is a region of many peoples and many cultures. The colonially created nations have separated some, brought others together but in generally weak states which are further enfeebled by ethnic or regional aspirations. Expressed on a larger political stage those aspirations are likely to be less disruptive. West African leaders now face a contradictory challenge: to strengthen and yet also transcend these young nations.

THIRTEEN

ACCRA ENCOUNTERS

That evening, having earlier failed in my assault on the Castle, I wandered into an Accra bar. Overhearing me order a drink, a man standing beside me mistook my accent for that of an American and said, 'Hey, man, what's the news from New York?' I glanced at him suspiciously: he had an unkempt goatee beard, wore thick plastic-framed glasses, a shiny, frayed, brown safari suit, and was so skinny he seemed unsteady on his feet for want of nourishment. 'Haven't a clue, mate,' I muttered. To which he replied, extending a hand, smiling widely through his beard: 'Kofi Taylor, graduate of the University of London, former resident of Hampstead'.

So we got talking. I told him about my journey. He told me about his years in London. Kofi was a man constantly on the lookout for the main chance. He said he could arrange for me to interview Jerry Rawlings or Kwesi Botchwey, the Finance Minister. 'They were my classmates. I drink with them all the time,' he tried to assure me. With a loquacity which ignored my obvious scepticism, Kofi proceeded to imply that he was occasionally called up to serve the government in 'matters of vital national interest'.

I had nothing to lose. I gave him my hotel details and we parted, with him warning me that I could be called any time for an interview, even the middle of the night. Two days later Kofi Taylor turned up at the hotel. He looked morose, depressed, not in the least like a man who enjoyed night-

caps with the powers that be. He wasted no time in letting me
know that he was broke. Broke, because in pursuit of 'our
contract', he had had to make an outlay to his 'man in the
Castle'.

I said I wasn't aware that we had made a contract, and he
settled for a double whisky. The hotel barman knew Kofi and,
as we drank, several foreigners, business-types, greeted him.
It later became clear to me that Kofi made his living by smooth-
ing the passage of foreign businessmen. But I had to deduce
this from a conversation which meandered from his days in
Hampstead to the contemporary relevance of Maoism to Africa,
and the vanguardism of the PNDC. 'I'm not saying these guys
are getting it right,' Kofi said. 'But they're trying. You know,
in Nkrumah's time they defined socialism as "You chop—I
chop". Not these guys.'

From the hotel we drove to an open-air nightclub near
Kwame Nkrumah Circle. Here an unseen DJ harshly warned
that people who were not drinking, but occupying tables and his
valuable dance floor space, should either leave or spend money.
Surprisingly, people did actually order more drinks in response
to his angry, tyrannical voice.

As neither of us liked the nightclub, we drove on to a bar
beside the sea. It was here that Kofi told me about his return
to Ghana after many years in London. Exactly what he did in
London, following his studies, was a mystery. The most he
would say was this: 'I was a Black man; I manipulated and I was
open to manipulation.'

Soon after Rawlings' second coup, Kofi decided that the
'beautiful ones were now born' (an allusion to the novel of political disenchantment, *The Beautiful Ones Are Not Yet Born*, by
the Ghanaian writer Ayi Kwei Armah). 'I wanted to be part of
the revolution.'

Within weeks of re-entering the country, he had secured an
office in the Castle as a PR man for the revolutionary council.
The country was in the grip of a euphoria which made an African
utopia seem possible. But one day, in a public meeting, Kofi
spoke out against the revolution's cultural nationalist tendency.
'They wanted to play only traditional Ghanaian music on the

radio. I said they were crazy. Have you heard Ghanaian music? It's all dirges.'

He was roundly booed, and some members of the revolution started asking questions about him: where had he come from, how had he managed to get an office in the Castle when stalwart supporters of the revolution were still seeking a niche? One morning Kofi woke up in prison, his head shaved, his body aching and bruised, and under suspicion for spying.

But Kofi survived, forgave, and made his peace with the revolutionaries. He seemed a pragmatic, resilient man who survived entirely on his wits; a man who lived close to death but would die somewhere peacefully at a moment when he chose, an empty whisky bottle and an empty glass at his bedside.

I next saw Kofi in the hotel lobby. He introduced to me the man he was talking to, an Englishman from Bristol who worked for a shipping company. But Kofi's preoccupied air hastened my departure. He promised to call; and though I asked several times, there was never a message from him at the hotel reception desk.

The hotel itself was a characterless glass cube designed for business travellers, and managed by French expatriates. Its one redeeming feature comprised two tennis courts, on which you could get coaching lessons from a sparky, smiling coach or his dull assistant.

The final quarrel of the journey, and certainly the most bitter, occurred on the tennis court. Noah and I had begun to learn tennis in the mornings in Yaoundé. We resumed here. Late one evening, under floodlights, we played a match umpired by the coach's assistant, who stood by the net. At some stage of the game I noticed that the umpire was shouting the score only to my opponent. When I asked him the score, I thought I heard him say: 'Your master fifteen, you forty.'

I could not believe my ears and so asked him again. He repeated the same words. I was stunned with incredulity and indignation. This was Ghana 1990! Ghana, once the shining star of African independence! Ghana, where most African-Jamaicans originated from, where the names of early Jamaican freedom fighters like Kojo and Taki and Nana were everyday names. I played the remainder of the game in a fever of angry astonishment. When the match finished, I called him aside fully intending to roast him in the flames of a fury enhanced by adrenalin, unappeased by my victory. I glaringly asked whether it had ever occurred to him that my companion and I might be colleagues; had he never seen a black and white person in an equal relationship? He stubbornly denied that he had used the word 'master', which further angered me. I called him a 'lying Uncle Tom', and walked away.

For the next three days I refused to speak to him, or have him coach me: I glowered fiercely when our paths crossed. He must have complained to his boss, because the coach attempted to act as a mediator, relaying and reiterating his assistant's denial. After hearing me out the coach called his assistant to finally settle the matter. But the assistant persisted with his mendacity. Recognising that the situation was irresolvable I vented my spleen by calling him a lying bushman and an escapee from a Tarzan movie, and left it at that.

This altercation with the coach's assistant gave me no pleasure and was as disconcerting as all the other quarrels and squabbles of what had too often seemed like a fractious dash round West Africa. In preceding incidents I had regained my equilibrium in the solitude of my room, or usually, by the sea. In Accra I went to church. Since arriving I had noticed a quaint little old Anglican church and now decided to go there. I did not go because I am an Anglican or religious but because, I suppose, I am one of those people whose anger, however justified, is frequently followed by a degree of remorse. The tranquillity of a church has the same comforting effect as the sea.

I approached the church door at the same time as an elderly gentleman and we discovered together that it was locked. Separately we walked to a kiosk under a tamarind tree within the churchyard. There I bought a cold drink, and sat on a bench. The old man did the same, and we soon struck up a conversation.

He would be travelling to Kumasi later in the day and felt a special need to pray. He was gravely disappointed that the church was closed.

On learning that his surname was Cole, I asked how he had come by the name. He said that his great-grandfather had been a migrant from Sierra Leone, a Creole. Mr Cole, however, saw himself as a hundred per cent Ghanaian, as were his mother and grandmother.

He had another reason for wishing to pray that morning. He had woken up worried about his children. He had two boys and a girl living in London. They had originally gone there as students, but were now working. 'What is there to come back to?' he asked rhetorically. 'They are young. There's no work here.' But he was concerned that they might not be able to live in Ghana again. He said that in each new letter he discerned a small sign of change. A tone, a way of expression, minor hints of a changing way of seeing the world.

The most I could say was that his foreparents had probably been absent for generations but they still returned.

Then he revealed the real source of his anxiety, the distressing possibility that he might never see those children again.

I had no words of consolation and for a long while there was a strangely intimate silence between us. Then he laughed lightly and said: 'Don't let an old man burden you with his worries.'

We talked for a while longer in a lighter mood. Then I had to leave for my first interview of the day. As I stood, he asked when I would be travelling to Britain.

I said I would be 'going back home to London' on tomorrow evening's flight. I walked away and the echo of my own answer rang with a note of falseness. I began to realise then that I had no home to which I could return, no place to which I belonged. My numerous visits to Africa since 1979 expressed and heightened my awareness of that personal dilemma but could not resolve it.

I caught a taxi immediately outside the church grounds. As it pulled away, I glanced at the sad old man who was still seated on the bench in the churchyard, his head in his hands, ruminating under the tamarind tree, and I felt relieved that I would soon be leaving this Africa which so often and with such intensity made me feel like an orphan of history.

POSTSCRIPT: RETURN TO NIGERIA

There appear to have been many changes in West Africa since my 1990 journey. Inspired by events in Eastern Europe and encouraged by Western governments' insistence on greater democracy as a condition for future economic aid, West Africans – reflecting trends elsewhere on the continent – have over the past two years taken to the streets demanding an end to military or one-party rule. The people have tasted independence. Now they want democracy.

In Cameroon, months of mass protests – in which the country's Anglophone minority played a leading role – forced Paul Biya's regime to allow the existence of opposition parties. Political parties are also in the process of being created in Ghana, where Jerry Rawlings' government has finally conceded to the resumption of civilian rule. If Ghana's transition programme goes according to plan, the country should have an elected government by the end of 1992. Adu Boahen, the retired historian whom I interviewed in Accra in 1990, has emerged as a key figure in the debate about Ghana's democratic future.

Sierra Leone was also affected by the popular demand for democracy which swept through Africa from the latter half of 1990. President Joseph Momoh was one of the first one-party rulers to accede to these demands. However, Momoh did not survive in power long enough to oversee the transition to multi-party politics. In April 1992, confronted with unrest in the junior ranks of the army, he fled to Guinea, and on 29th April Captain Valentine Strasser created the National Provisional Ruling Council and assumed control as chairman.

Momoh's fall was partly caused by events in neighbouring

Liberia. The invasion – led by Charles Taylor – which had begun three weeks before my arrival in Monrovia had not been crushed by the Samuel Doe government. Rather it had escalated swiftly into a terrible civil war which turned Monrovia into a bloodbath and threatened to destabilise the entire West African region. In an unprecedented move, the Economic Community of West African States intervened in the war, despatching troops drawn from member states to Monrovia. These troops, known as the Ecomog forces, brought the war to a stalemate but did not end it. Taylor still controls most of Liberia, except Monrovia.

The presence of the Ecomog forces together with a split in the ranks of the invading army enabled President Samuel Kanyon Doe to remain in nominal control of the Liberian state. But not for long. In a series of confusing events, Doe was captured and tortured to death by a faction of the insurgent forces – led by the bizarre figure of Prince Johnson – in September 1990. It is rumoured that videos of Doe's execution were circulating amongst exiled Liberians in Europe and America weeks later.

The Nigerian army provided the largest number of troops in the Ecomog forces, bolstering that country's leadership status in Africa. But domestic events in Nigeria since 1990 suggest that it will be many years before Nigeria fully assumes the leadership role in sub-Saharan Africa that its size and population merits. In April 1990, a coup attempt led by middle-ranking officers almost toppled the Babangida regime. Seizing control of the Lagos Radio station, they recited the usual litany of reasons for the coup – corruption, economic mismanagement – but went one step further than previous coup leaders by announcing the excision of five northern states from the federation. Had the coup succeeded, the country probably would have descended into a civil war yet again. Fortunately, it was quashed within a few days and Nigeria remains intact and on course to full civil rule by December 1992.

Nigeria's civilian rulers will be faced, however, with a monumental task, with the military – the commitment of which to democracy, at least in the ranks below the generals, is uncertain – looking over their shoulders. Not only is national unity still tenuous, but social divisions have worsened. Since 1990, thousands of people have been killed in social disturbances in cities throughout the federation – Kano, Borno, Katsina, Sokoto and Lagos. Religious and ethnic intolerance played no small part in these urban massacres. But so too did the economic hardship faced by Nigerian city dwellers who are forced to live in overcrowded unsanitary accommodation and eke out a livelihood in an economic climate created largely by the prescriptions of Western financial institutions. Policies like Nigeria's Structural Adjustment Programme have social and political repercussions which cold-hearted economists in the World Bank and the IMF dismiss as irrelevant. It seems to me, for instance, that however real the animosity between ethnic groups or Muslims and Christians, the violence that has wracked Nigerian cities in recent years cannot be disassociated from that country's – and the African continent's – economic state.

None the less, the changes which have occurred since 1990 are not negligible. They signal a new mood and the emergence of new actors on the political stage. These new leaders emerging out of what could be described as Africa's second wind of change will be judged by their ability to steer the ship of state through a treacherous economic sea which has dashed the hopes of the independence generations and claimed many well-meaning rulers. People, to paraphrase Marx, make history but not in circumstances of their own choosing.

*　　*　　*

Africa, of course, is not only a continent of young states grappling with the multifarious problems of development. It is a vital cultural reference point for people of African ancestry in the West. That Africa, Africa as cultural symbol, is perhaps stronger today than it has ever been in the past. The continent is a continuing source of fascination and inspiration to its descendants in the West. In this infinitely smaller world on the

eve of the millennium, ideas, art and cultural practices are flowing to and fro between Africa and the New World. For example,
Kwanzaa – an end of year celebration which began in the United
States – has become part of the annual calendar in many communities in the USA and Britain. And the intelligentsia of such
communities increasingly talk of Afrocentricity, a world view
which asserts the primacy of things African, from clothes to
ideas, from figures like Malcolm X to the Senegalese historian
Cheikh Anta Diop.

This reclamation of Africa is likely to be given fresh impetus
by a new movement born out of the increased contact between
Africans on the continent and African descendants, and out of
Africa's debt problems and the disadvantages which African
descendants in the West continue to suffer. Known as the Reparation Movement, it is still young but has many influential
supporters, including the Organisation of African Unity and the
Black Caucus of the United States Congress. Furthermore, it
believes it has an unassailable moral, legal and historical case:

'Slavery and colonialism have inflicted tremendous damage
on Africa and on Africans in the diaspora. Millions of Africans
have died in the process of implementation of these policies,
the African economy, culture and societies were completely
devastated. For over four hundred and fifty years Africans
were caught, manacled and shipped across the Atlantic to
create wealth in other parts of the world. Those who did not
die during the raids or in transit were condemned to lives of
servitude. The millions captured were the young and virile
Africans, the very class needed for development of the continent. Slavery was accompanied and later replaced by colonialism. Many more millions died resisting colonialism. The
curtailment of freedom and the disruption of the normal way
of life of the Africans created psychological, social, economic
and political problems, the scars of which are still with us. It
is for these damages and injustices that reparation is sought.'
(The Report of the World Conference on Reparation to Africa
and Africans in the Diaspora, Lagos 1990.)

The practicalities of exacting reparation from Western countries, whose current level of economic and technological development would not have occurred without the exploitation of Africa's peoples and resources, have not been worked out. But whether the movement succeeds seems immaterial: it is the potential for unifying Africans everywhere which excites one of its leading figures, Dudley Thompson, the Jamaican High Commissioner to Nigeria. I met him in May 1992, in Lagos, when I returned to Nigeria. A short, round, pugnacious man, he described himself as a proud pan-Africanist in the tradition of Marcus Garvey, Ras Makonnen, George Padmore and Kwame Nkrumah. As a barrister, he had defended Jomo Kenyatta in the Mau Mau trials in Kenya.

I passed an enlightening and entertaining evening with His Excellency on the ninth floor of the Eko Hotel, Victoria Island. The hotel overlooks the Atlantic Ocean and out there in the darkness, an electric storm intermittently illuminated the night sky in cracking bursts of light. Around the table were a Scot, Douglas Eadie, and an Englishman, Ian Taylor. They were producer and director respectively of the project which had brought me here: writing and presenting a documentary for Channel Four television about me journeying from Kano to Lagos.

His Excellency had been in the RAF in the Second World War and had something of the British bulldog spirit about him. He certainly bit Douglas and Ian. He reminded them of Britain's 'iniquitous' past in the slave trade and colonialism. Speaking for the Reparation Movement, in an accent redolent of Oxford and upper-class Jamaica, Mr Thompson said: 'Justice will only be done to the Africans when our contribution to civilisation is acknowledged by the West.'

They shifted uneasily in their seats, their guilt as glaring as the occasional flashes of light. Had I been judge and jury I would have passed the heaviest sentence permitted by the statute book and retired to bed feeling infinitely better because a shameful wrong had finally been righted.

The evening took on a lighter note when Mr Thompson, who believes his African roots lay in Ghana, proudly revealed that his grandfather was Scottish. This in turn led to a bitterly amusing exchange between producer and director, between the Scotsman and the Englishman in which the former reminded the latter of England's injustices in Scotland. Naturally, I fuelled the argument.

Some days after that dinner we – director, producer and myself – left a Lagos torn by rioting and travelled by car to Ife, Oshogbo, Benin City, Lokoja, Abuja, Kaduna, Zaria and Kano. At this last stop, the film crew, all Scots, joined us. The return journey to Lagos, from savannah to forest to sea, from Muslim north to the predominantly Christian south, would be the film.

It was an eventful journey (the full details of which would require another book altogether to describe), in which I sailed down the Niger; drove through landscapes dotted with ant-hills which looked like cathedrals; prostrated myself before the Ooni of Ife; worshipped at a Shrine to Osun, the goddess of water; and was praised one Sunday afternoon on Leke beach by a band of drumming praise-singers, the Atlantic beating a not discordant rhythm on the shore, my stomach purring from a lunch of egusi fish and pounded yam beside a Lagos lagoon.

All this, while several Nigerian cities were being torn by civil unrest. Most of these disturbances were quite clearly protests against the government's harsh economic policies, which had two months earlier led to a forty per cent depreciation of the naira. The resultant price rises, exacerbated by hoarding and fuel scarcity, increased the cost of basic commodities beyond most people's pockets. Discontent saturated the cities.

The highlight of this trip was revisiting Ahmadu Bello University in Zaria, where I had lived and worked for two years. I did not go there expecting to meet old friends because I knew they had all long moved on, my African-American friends back to various parts of the New World or elsewhere in Africa, my African and Nigerian friends to more lucrative positions outside academia. I went looking for memories, memories of love and youth and those stillborn dreams that one always recalls with a sweet melancholy.

The campus is especially beautiful during the rainy season.

And the rains had started. Flame trees blazed on the savannah, mango trees were laden with fruit and the vines had begun to sprout from the yam mounds. Even the baobab tree was in bloom, its roots like branches – bare in the dry season, giving it the appearance of an upside down tree – draped in the light green of newly sprouted leaves. But the preceding decade had ravaged the campus. The faculty building in which I had worked now looked like a slum tenement and the lecture rooms and theatres were empty but for a few students who had chosen to remain on campus though the university was closed for classes. The result of a student strike months before.

Lecturers were also preparing to strike to press their demand for higher salaries and more resources. I met a few former colleagues, those who had resisted the temptation to escape the perennial shortage of books, appalling salaries and recurrent disruption of the academic year for better paid work in the private sector or abroad.

The senior staff club, once daily filled with the clinking of beer bottles and the clash of ideas and theories, was now a ghostly place where a few seemingly tired academics discussed, without vigour, the eternal crisis of Africa. When I asked one former colleague what had happened to the vibrant debates which used to occur here, he said gravely: 'Ah, my friend, have you not heard? The age of ideas is over, history is finished. This is the age of money.'

A statement like that in this setting a decade before would have sparked a discussion which would have ended temporarily with the closing of the staff club, resumed the following afternoon and eventually led to a seminar paper. Now it evinced a peculiar laughter, dispirited, resigned and yet somehow contemptuous.

Nevertheless, the few hours I spent on the ABU campus reaffirmed my belief that my life might have turned out entirely differently if I had not as a young man had the opportunity to work there. For two years this environment in which my colour was irrelevant had afforded me the space and time to reflect on my British upbringing, and what to do with my life. I had been both teacher and student. I had left ABU and academia determined to write, to survive outside the cosy, safe surroundings of institutions. A decade later I returned – as a writer.

A SELECT READING LIST

J. Omosade Awolalu, *Yoruba Beliefs and Sacrificial Rites* (Longman, London 1979)

Aimé Césaire, *Return to My Native Land* (Présence Africaine, Paris 1968 and Penguin, London 1969)

Cameron Duodu, *The Gab Boys* (Collins, London 1969)

C. L. R. James, *Nkrumah and the Ghana Revolution* (Allison & Busby, London 1977)

Charles S. Johnson, *Bitter Canaan: The Story of the Negro Republic* (Transaction Books, New Jersey 1957)

Hollis R. Lynch, *Edward Wilmot Blyden: Pan-Negro Patriot* (Oxford University Press, London 1967)

Kwame Nkrumah, *An Autobiography* (Thomas Nelson, Edinburgh 1957)

A. J. G. Wyse, *The Krios of Sierra Leone* (C. Hurst & Co, London 1989)

CHRISTINA DODWELL

TRAVELS WITH PEGASUS

An account of an exhilarating adventure across West Africa, from the Cameroun rain forest via the Sahara and Tombouctou. Christina Dodwell always chooses an unorthodox means of travel, but the microlight is the most unusual yet. As well as the danger involved it also had the great advantage of getting her to areas inaccessible to ground transport and allowing her to land wherever she wished to explore.

She met duck-billed women, pygmies, a mountain sorceror, dancers and nomads. She canoed on Lake Chad, flew through a dust storm, rode a camel into the Aïr Mountains and – most memorable of all her many adventures – discovered a dinosaur graveyard.

'Will be as fascinating to the general non-fiction reader as to the converted travel book addict . . . The combination of problems in the air and adventure on the ground makes this one of the best travel books of the last twelve months'
The Oxford Times

'She is an observant traveller, respectful of local sensibilities and with a gift for being accepted in the most unlikely places'
The Times Literary Supplement

'Christina Dodwell is one of those intrepid British female explorers in the great tradition that stretches from Mary Kingsley to Freya Stark'
Daily Express

GEORGE PACKER

THE VILLAGE OF WAITING

'In 1982–1983 George Packer worked for the Peace Corps as an English teacher in the village of Lavié in Togo, West Africa, and here recounts his occasionally comic, more often poignant, and frequently tragic experiences in sharp, descriptive prose. He writes with an honest sense of realism, presenting a full view of Togolese customs and society, exploring such topics as work, medical care, marriage and sex, politics, drought and tourists. He is at his best when he writes about people, revealing their histories and psychologies with great sympathy and care'
Publishers Weekly

'Excellent . . . It's about how one tiny bit of the Third World works – and how it doesn't work. It's also about a painful and overwhelming experience of coming of age in a strange country. It strikes one immediately as both truthful and perceptive'
James Fenton

'The author doesn't pretend to know it all, but he knows plenty, and shares it with grace and humour in this colourful and disturbing book about contemporary West Africa'
Kirkus Reviews

'Both lovely in its feeling for the people he met there and realistic in its assessment of the African situations . . . A first-rate piece of social reportage'
Irving Howe

sceptre

DENNISON BERWICK

AMAZON

Venturing alone into the Amazon basin, Dennison Berwick travelled 4,000 miles along the river and its tributaries to explore man's relationship with untamed nature. In this absorbing account of a journey beset as much by comic accidents as by danger, he describes his extraordinary encounter with the Yanomami Indians and brings colourfully to life the landscape, peoples and plight of the world's last great wilderness.

'Offers riveting portrayals of the spectacular beauty and variety in the region'
Tam Dalyell in The Sunday Times

'Despite brushes with blow darts, piranha and vicious rapids, he still finds fine words when lost in the spirit of the jungle . . . The tale of the journey is told humbly and well. And more, Berwick's vision is acute'
Sandy Mitchell in Country Life

'Thoughtful and vastly entertaining . . . Berwick lets the land and its people speak for themselves'
Norman Cook in the Liverpool Daily Post

'Superbly written . . . Evocative and humorous, this is a classic piece of travel writing'
Lucy Harrington in the Hampstead and Highgate Express

'Captivating and exhilarating . . . as much a fascinating and timely record of the people of the rainforest as it is the story of a personal quest'
Isabel Walker in Traveller

sceptre

PETER SOMERVILLE-LARGE

A SHAGGY YAK STORY

In the 1950s, Peter Somerville-Large taught Milton to Afghan army cadets in Kabul before venturing into the remotest parts of Central Asia, hunting tiger in Nepal and being arrested in Bhutan. In this enchanting account of his travels he recreates a world untouched by tourism or the Kalashnikov, contrasting it with the experience of recent returns and his expedition to restore yaks to a tribe of refugee Kirghiz.

'Skilfully weaves together recent journeys in Pakistan and experiences during the 1950s . . . shot through with nostalgia for a vanished age of travel and witty'
The Daily Telegraph

'Englishmen are famous for their romantic lunacy in the East, but they've got nothing on the Irish'
The Observer

'Marked by the same verve, the same humour, the same insatiable curiosity about people and places, that gave his earlier books their unique flavour'
Irish Independent

'Engrossing. I enjoyed every page of this larger than life tale'
The Irish Times

'Informative, funny and guaranteed to ignite the wander lust in even the most geographically apathetic, this book is a great story and a marvellous read. Highly recommended'
Dublin Evening Press

LESLEY DOWNER

ON THE NARROW ROAD TO THE DEEP NORTH

In 1689 Matsuo Basho, Japan's greatest poet, set out on his last and longest journey, to the remote northern provinces. His moving account, rich in strange and sometimes comic encounters along the road, is the most famous and much loved work in Japanese literature.

Three hundred years later, inspired by Basho's writing and her passion for Japan, Lesley Downer set off in his footsteps. Walking and hitchhiking towards the Sacred Mountains with their legendary hermit priests, meeting people who had never seen a Westerner and dining on flowers and sautéed grasshoppers, she discovered a world which many Japanese believe vanished centuries ago.

'She is the perfect guide – expert, intrepid, following a dream'
John Carey in The Sunday Times

'One of the principal charms of ON THE NARROW ROAD TO THE DEEP NORTH is that it deals with aspects of Japan which are quite outside any of our stereotyped assumptions . . . Downer has an instinctive insight into the way the Japanese think – a rare commodity which she uses with a marvellous delicacy of touch'
Katie Hickman in The Literary Review

sceptre